Seeking the Pearl of Great Price

My Life as a Counter-Cultural Catholic

Fae Stuart Presley

Copyright © 2022 by Fae D. Presley or Timothy S. Presley
All rights reserved.
Cover image: dreamstime

Excerpts from the English translation of the *Catechism of the Catholic Church* for use in the United States of America copyright © 1994, United States Catholic Conference, Inc.—Libreria Editrice Vaticana. English translation of the *Catechism of the Catholic Church: Modifications from the Editio Typica* copyright © 1997, United States Conference of Catholic Bishops—Libreria Editrice Vaticana.

No part of this book may be reproduced, stored in a retrieval system, or transmitted in any form, or by any means, electronic, mechanical, photocopying, or otherwise, without the prior written permission of the author or copyright holder, except by a reviewer, who may quote brief passages for review.

Additional copies of this book are available at lulu.com.

Imprint: Lulu.com
ISBN 978-1-312-53679-1

For my children and grandchildren

and all those who follow

This is how we came to live the Catholic faith in our family.
May you remain faithful and courageous in this
one, holy, catholic, and apostolic Church.

CONTENTS

Introduction	9
1 Cows, Chores, and Church	11
2 Courtship With a Catholic?!	35
3 Surprised by the Spirit	53
4 Faith and Fertility	69
5 Infant to Toddler to School Age…Then What?	88
6 Alaska, North Dakota, and Three New Christians	99
7 On the Move…Again	120
8 Glorifying God in Our Family Life—Sometimes Yes, Sometimes No	135
9 Pray Always	156
10 Why Does the Sun Go on Shining?	180
11 Mostly Cloudy or Partly Sunny?	206
12 Joy and Anguish in the Heat of Texas	234
13 Jesus, I Trust in You Even More	246
14 Only One Thing is Necessary	263
15 A Carmelite Path to the Pearl of Great Price	277
Epilogue	287
Appendices:	
#1 Ed Stuart's Family Tree	297
#2 Bible Quiz for Bible Christians	299
#3 My Father's Briefcase	307
#4 A Tribute to Ed Stuart From His Family	313
#5 Favorite Scripture Verses	325
Acknowledgments	329

Introduction

"Proclaim the greatness of the Lord with me; let us extol His name together."
~ *Psalm 34:4*

This is the story of an ordinary life. There is a song that often played in our home when my children were young entitled, *Juan Diego*. (St. Juan Diego was the privileged seer of our Blessed Virgin Mary in Mexico in 1531.) He sings, "I was an ordinary man, living in ordinary times, an ordinary life…making rugs out of reeds with Maria Lucia, my wife." Working simply while living with his wife, yet God, through our Blessed Mother, did profound things in his life!

I am not a seer nor a mystic nor a saint, but God has done marvelous things in my ordinary life. I want everyone to know God does amazing things in all of our lives if we have a willing spirit and open our hearts to Him.

Writing a memoir is fraught with potential disaster. I'm not only telling my own story, but also stories of family members and friends, whom I love. And none of us is perfect! There are no perfect parents or families or churchmen. I do not reveal all of my life's dirt…nor anyone else's…but try to give an accurate picture of the struggles, questions, and pitfalls that have been part of my life. My family and friends could write their own memoirs and their stories about our shared experiences would be different. These are my memories, my beliefs, and my feelings.

April 2021   Fae Presley

1
Cows, Chores, and Church

The doctor's voice on the phone that Friday afternoon was slow and deliberate. "The test shows a mass in your husband's brain. You need to make an appointment with a neurologist as soon as possible."

As my mind struggled to accept this news, the tears quietly formed and began to run down my face. I made my way blindly up the stairs to where my husband lay in our bedroom. I knelt by the bed, placing my hand on his arm. "That was the doctor calling. There's a mass in your brain."

He calmly said, "Well, after all this time, now we know what it is."

Returning downstairs, I gathered the youngest three of our five children who still lived at home and tried to explain as calmly as I could what was happening with their father. I felt a great need to pray, to pray the prayer about which Pope St. John Paul II said, "… should be for every Christian and even more so for Christian families, a spiritual oasis during the day from which to get courage and confidence."[1] I very much needed courage and confidence as the children and I began the

---

[1] John Paul II, Angelus in Otranto, Italy, Oct. 5, 1980 as quoted in *In Conversation with God*, Vol. 4, p. 559.

1 Cows, Chores, and Church

sorrowful mysteries of our Blessed Mother's rosary. Our family's sorrowful mysteries began in earnest that day in late summer of 2002, but oh, how I see the hand of God through it all. In fact, God's mercy has followed me all of my life, as unbeknownst even to myself, I have sought the pearl of great price.

> *"Again, the kingdom of heaven is like to a merchant seeking good pearls. Who, when he had found one pearl of great price, went and sold all that he had and bought it."*
> Matthew 13:45-46

I grew up on a dairy farm with my parents and two older brothers about two miles away from my paternal grandparent's farm. My grandparents were the second generation to farm those 160 acres in Michigan, raising dairy cows, sheep, pigs, chickens, and growing lush and large gardens. My grandmother, Grandma Alice, attended church every week and was active there, along with placing much importance on reading the Bible every day. I remember going to church with her occasionally and attending Vacation Bible School at the Pilgrim Holiness Church in our nearby town.

My grandfather, George, did not attend church while I knew him, so my father, Ronald, grew up in a divided home in regards to faith. Grandpa George was a fun-loving man in my child's eyes, even though he worked very hard all day. In the evenings, it would be a treat to watch while he peeled apples for us kids and the peels would stretch from the apple all the way down to the floor as we tried to gobble them up.

Grandma Alice was very special to me. She taught me many things as she went about her duties on the farm and in her home. I wrote a poem about her after I had grown up and married.

To My Grandma

Her house down the road
Was a favorite, wonderful place.
A cool front porch in the summer sun,
A warm and toasty wood stove when
The snow tumbled down.

Just a bike ride away,
She was always there.
Maybe in the chicken coop,
Maybe in the garden;
Mowing the yard or
Weeding the flowers.

Her candy and cookies, I'll admit

1   Cows, Chores, and Church

Were tempting,
But so were Thanksgiving and
Christmas potatoes and dressing.

Treasured memories of eating
Apple peels, sleeping on the living room
Couch or upstairs
In "my" room,
Cleaning chicken gizzards,
Picking grapes and pears and apricots,
The smell of a new clothes
Dryer in the basement.

Oh, yes, the basement—
row after row of canned jars,
With pickles and pears, peaches
And jam. Potatoes with long
Eyes in the bin, and a
Freezer with a door that would bite!

My grandma was a friend
To me then; in my child eyes,
Just my grandma.

But then I got married—

1   Cows, Chores, and Church

Even that too, in her front yard,
With purple and white lilacs,
Sparkling spirea and golden
Forsythia. Her house
Wasn't down the road
Anymore; indeed, she didn't
Live there anymore.
She moved to town, and
I moved away.

Today, she's not just
My grandma.
We've grown closer as
I've grown older.

A trusted friend, a wise
Counselor, a listening ear,
A playful pal, and a
Patient teacher.

My grandma is all this to me, and
I love her so.

 Farmers in those days worked so hard. When I was a young mother myself, Grandma Alice admired the fact that my husband, Ed, and I homeschooled our children. One day we were talking about homeschooling and she sighed and said, "Oh, there was always so much work to do." To me this meant, "I would have liked to homeschool too, but there was too much work to do." (Grandma Alice had taught many grades and subjects in one-room schoolhouses before her first child was born.)

My father, Ronald, was also a hard-working farmer. His pride and joy was his herd of registered Holstein dairy cows, a top-producing herd in the county. But he also had a tender heart. I believe he struggled to hide his emotions, as any strong farmer would in those days. Even though he did not verbalize love for me, I know he loved me. We were like the family in Pearl S. Buck's story, "Christmas Day in the Morning." A farm family, like mine; the 15-year-old son was awakened every morning at four o'clock to help with milking the cows. One Christmas morning he was awake early. He heard his father speak to his mother, lamenting that he had to wake the boy so early. "When he heard these words, something in him woke: his father loved him! He had never thought of it before, taking for granted the tie of their blood. Neither his father nor his mother talked about loving their children—they had no time for such things. There was always so much to do on a farm."² This is how I grew up.

I remember an incident though that still consoles me. A rite of passage on the farm was raising a calf to show at the county fair. My calf was named Misty and I was very attached to her. One morning my father came in from doing chores and told me Misty had died in the barnyard. He held me in his arms as I sobbed. That was the first time I remember feeling his love and comfort.

He did not attend church during the years of my early childhood. My mother, Floy, would occasionally take us to the Methodist Church. I remember singing and learning many hymns in the choir my mother directed.

There was always work to do. I had many chores, including feeding the calves (lots of them), cleaning cow stalls and bedding them with straw, scraping manure off walkways, cleaning the milking parlor, milking cows, working with hay in the summer, driving tractor and working up fields, pulling weeds in the garden and mowing the lawn.

It seems that physical labor is shunned today and seen almost as an evil to be avoided at all costs. In the beginning, before Adam's fall, work "was not yet a burden, but rather the

---

² Pearl S. Buck, "Christmas Day in the Morning," in *Home for Christmas—Stories for Young and Old*, ed. Miriam LeBlanc (Walden, New York: Plough Publishing House, 2014), 67.

collaboration of man and woman with God in perfecting the visible creation."[3] In a real sense, farming is involved explicitly with this goal of perfecting creation, drawing forth from the goods of the earth abundant fruit. Even now, with our "tainted nature," work "honors the Creator's gifts and the talents received from Him. By enduring the hardship of work …man collaborates in a certain fashion with the Son of God in His redemptive work."[4] Actually, "the refusal to work is a form of theft since it robs the human community of necessary human resources, deprives it of gifts God has given, and all the while still draws on the fruits of others' labors."[5] I am so thankful for my early life as a child on the farm. While I did not appreciate the work demands then, I realize now the great gift that was given me as the value of physical labor was planted deep within me.

We did have lots of fun on the farm too. We had a small John Deere 420 tractor. In the winter, on the back of the tractor, we hooked up a rubber belt from an old chopper wagon. (This is a large, enclosed wagon which chopped corn or hay is blown into by another implement called a chopper.

---

[3] *Catechism of the Catholic Church,* 2nd Ed., (Washington, DC: United States Catholic Conference, 2000), par. 378.

[4] *CCC,* par. 2427.

[5] Msgr. Charles Pope, *The Ten Commandments,* (Charlotte, NC: TAN Books, 2014), 57.

1 Cows, Chores, and Church

To empty the wagon, a conveyor belt pushes the chopped crops, called silage, out the side of the wagon.) The belt was wide enough that we could sit on it and hold on to the edges while my oldest brother, Randy, pulled us around the circular driveway on the snow. When he went around the corners, we would fly way out and it was very exciting! One day the neighbor kids had come over, and one of them was riding alone. Unfortunately, Randy cut the corner too close and the belt went down into the ditch and smashed the neighbor boy up pretty good. He wasn't really hurt…probably a bit sore… and we had a good laugh about it later.

Another fun memory was hanging on for dear life as I soared through the air. There was a silo next to the barn, about 30' tall. Part of the equipment to fill the silo with silage was a rope with a pulley on the top of the silo. A propane tank sat next to the silo, and there was a small building on the other side of the silo with a roof about 10' high. Randy and Ken, my other brother, got the idea to have me stand on the propane tank holding one end of the rope while they stood on the ground and pulled the other end of the rope. Of course, I went up in the air nearly to the top of the silo. Then they'd let me down and I'd land on the roof of the nearby building.

My brothers and I liked to play popular board games. I liked to take long walks with our Chihuahua dog, Max, exploring all the woods and fields around our farm. I went on

1   Cows, Chores, and Church

bike rides too, for many miles. It was a time when parents didn't have to worry about kids out and about so much. I was alone often, as there was only one neighbor who was a girl and her family and ours didn't associate much together.

My favorite memory of fun as a child though, was playing softball. My father was an excellent pitcher in high school. He could have played college ball, but chose to study farming instead at Michigan State University. He loved the game, and when young, he always listened to the Detroit Tigers play on the radio when he could…which wasn't very often, so he asked Grandma Alice to listen and tell him about it. He taught his three children to play and made a ball diamond on our yard. In between the circular driveway was the perfect spot. He built a backstop and we had bases. On the evenings that we planned a game, we had to start milking the cows early so we'd be done and still have time to play. The neighbor kids would all come over so we had plenty of players. I can still see my father standing there, leaning against the backstop, watching us, giving tips, grinning and enjoying himself. I kept my baseball glove for many years, and even played on an adult team when my oldest son was just a baby. I wasn't a pro, but I sure did enjoy it. I was usually sore after playing as an adult!

A particular source of enjoyment as a child at home was reading. I would try to hide when I read so nobody would see

1 Cows, Chores, and Church

me and ask me why I wasn't doing something! I dreaded hearing the outside door shut…it meant someone (usually Randy) had come in the house and was looking for me to get to work! We didn't have many children's books though, and I had no way to go to the library. I didn't even know what a library was as a child, and I don't remember ever being in a library until I was in high school. I got some books of my own to read through the Scholastic Book Club in 7th and 8th grades. The teachers would pass out a flyer listing the books for sale, along with pictures and descriptions and prices. I spent my own money on these books, earned doing chores. I still have one of them that was a favorite, *The Velvet Room*.

Other childhood adventures turned out to be not so much fun. I honestly wonder how I survived! When I was four or five years old, my family was over at my grandparents' farm. It was rainy, but the rain had stopped so my brothers and I were outside playing. Overhead electric wires were strung between two outbuildings and they hung down very low to the ground, low enough that I could actually reach them. The lower one was a ground wire and the top one was hot. I was swinging away happily on the ground wire, swishing my bare feet in a mud puddle beneath me, when I thought, "I'm tall enough now to reach the top one!" I jumped up and grabbed the hot wire, which immediately sent 120 volts coursing through my body. I remember seeing my brothers playing

1 Cows, Chores, and Church

nearby. I watched my grandfather as he ran from the chicken coop, leaped over a fence, and putting one arm behind his back (which at that time was commonly believed to mitigate the effects of the electricity), grabbed me off the wire. I was unconscious by the time my grandfather reached me, but I remember waking up in my grandparents' house with my grandmother and mother huddled around me. I actually learned just recently that Randy had run over to me and grabbed me, but had experienced the shock himself and knew I was in big trouble. It was too difficult for him to free me from the wire, as the electricity causes the hands to clench tightly and he was not strong enough as a child to free me. He ran to the barn where my parents were milking cows but could not find them. He then ran to the chicken coop where my grandfather heard his shouts and came running. If it had not been for Randy's quick action, I may not have survived.

Then there was the time Randy had trained (or so he thought) a young bull to a yoke. We had an old horse-drawn implement; it was pretty rusty but still had wheels and seemed like it would work. My brother hitched up his bull to this implement and convinced me to sit in the metal seat on the back while he guided the bull. All was fine for a short while …but then the bull decided to have a little fun and took off with his tail in the air. The old implement couldn't take the sudden rush forward and the seat in which I was sitting broke

1 Cows, Chores, and Church

off and flew up in the air. I landed on the ground, still sitting on that seat. Yes, it did damage my backside and the injury was painful for many years.

Another brush with death occurred at the nearby creek. My brothers and I would ride our bikes two miles to the creek to swim and sometimes go fishing. Our fishing poles were long sticks. I don't remember what we used for line, but I remember the hooks, sticking the worms on them, and the bobbers and sinkers. One hot day I was swimming by myself, apart from the boys. The creek bed had some large rocks in it covered with moss that were quite slippery. Somehow I floundered on these rocks and kept falling under the water, over and over. I was gasping for air and the scenes of my short life flashed through my mind…I thought I was drowning. It must have been my guardian angel who eventually helped me find solid footing, and I carefully dragged myself out of the creek. I never mentioned this to anyone, but it influenced the rest of my life. I often prayed, "Oh, Lord, don't let me die by drowning!"

My brothers and I attended a one-room country school named Beverly School. It was just two miles from our farm. The school owned the cutest little bus, and my mother was our bus driver for some time. The bus had four seats, like regular bus seats, which seated two kids, down one side. On the other

1 Cows, Chores, and Church

side was a wooden bench that went from front to back, parallel with the windows.

There were six grades at the school then, with one teacher, but some years earlier 7th and 8th grades were included too. The teacher, Mrs. Bieth, thought since I could already read that it would be good for me to skip first grade. So I went from what was called "Beginners," to second grade and was thereafter in the same grade as my brother, Ken, through high school, though nearly two years younger.

There were about five of us in our grade, neighbors that we all knew. When it was time for our grade's lessons, we went up to a bench in the front of the room and sat down next to each other. There was a big blackboard on the wall in front of us and I remember going up to the board and writing arithmetic problems on it. (My parents retrieved one of those big blackboards when the school closed years later and hung it on their office wall.)

A "Bible Lady" used to come to school once a month to teach Bible lessons to all the Protestant children. The Catholic children were excused from this class and were allowed to go outside to play! I knew there was something different about those Catholic kids, but I didn't understand what the difference was, or why they were singled out.

My father, paternal grandfather, and maternal grandmother had all attended this same country school. Ken

1   Cows, Chores, and Church

and I were students there through fourth grade, which is when the school closed and we had to go to the consolidated school in town. I liked the country school very much, but I also enjoyed going to the school in town. Surprisingly, I fit in with the town kids and felt accepted and happy there for the fifth and sixth grades. One of the Catholic girls became a good friend but when my parents learned she was Catholic, they wouldn't let me visit her at her home.

I learned a valuable lesson in the sixth grade. Mrs. Bieth, the teacher from Beverly School, was teaching at our new school now and she was my teacher again. There was a very poor, disadvantaged girl in my class. She was always dirty and did not smell very good. It breaks my heart now to think of her. She did not have any friends, and to make matters worse, the group of girls that I was friends with regularly taunted her on the playground during recess. I only did it once, but soon, my friends and I were told to stay in during one recess period. Mrs. Bieth talked to us about what a clique is and what hurtful and shameful things a group like that can do. I never treated my classmate that way again and regretted my behavior long after.

Even though I lived on a farm with few personal material possessions, I didn't feel as though I was deprived. However, I did learn frugality. Trips to town were kept to a minimum and only when absolutely necessary. Lights were forbidden to be kept on when not needed. New clothes were bought only once a year before school began. Meals were simple farmer fare: meat (from our own animals), potatoes and vegetables grown in our garden, fruit from my grandparents' farm—rhubarb, pears, berries, apricots—and homemade cookies or pies. Lots of instant iced tea too, in the summer when haying was going on, and all the whole, raw milk we could drink.

My mother has always been a music lover, and, thankfully, she passed that on to me. She loved to sing and to direct church choirs. I remember going to sleep as a young child listening to her play the piano. When my parents could afford a stereo record player, I listened to her records of Beethoven's symphonies. I thought I had never heard anything so profoundly beautiful, and I marveled at God's grandeur, experienced through this music. I was able to take piano lessons myself for many years—I enjoyed playing Beethoven's *Moonlight Sonata*—and Ken and I both had voice lessons. This is remarkable as I think back on it. We lived on a small dairy farm, with income only from the sale of milk and no outside income, but my mother made sure there was enough money for music lessons.

Music became a large part of my life. I joined the school band in sixth grade and played the flute through high school and my first year of college. I really enjoyed marching band in high school. I sang in a small Christian band as a teenager and

1 Cows, Chores, and Church

I realized I enjoyed being in front of people, speaking or singing. My favorite song to perform was *My Tribute*, sung at that time by Andrae Crouch. A friend and I entered a church talent show as a duet and we competed at the state level, traveling to Calvin College in Grand Rapids. Later, I was also honored to sing at friends' weddings.

About this time, during my mid-teen years, my father began showing interest in faith in God. He decided our family would attend a Protestant church not far away. This was a bit difficult for my mother, as she was the choir director at a different church, but she likely was so thankful her husband wanted to attend church that she gave up her position so our whole family could be together. The pastor was quite charismatic and there were also some cute boys there, so I happily joined my family. I was baptized at this church, Lamotte Missionary Church, on October 17, 1971. I learned much about the Christian faith in those years and immersed myself in the Bible. We were regulars at Sunday School, Sunday morning worship, Sunday evening service, Wednesday night prayer meeting, and Friday night youth group.

This is where my search for truth began in earnest. I remember leaving an evening service with my parents one night. We were driving home, just the three of us, and I said (obviously having a crisis of faith!), "I just don't know how

1   Cows, Chores, and Church

you can believe in something you can't see!" Sadly, I don't remember my parents having an answer for me. It seemed they were unprepared to discuss their own experience of faith or reasons for belief. I probably wouldn't have accepted anything they might have said anyway! While I floundered then in my search for truth, God would provide the spark I needed in His own time.

When Ken and I were in the sixth grade, Randy was in the ninth grade, a freshman in high school. I don't know the details, but later I learned some of his classmates were trouble-makers and my parents were concerned. So they moved all of us the next year to a much larger school system. I was heartbroken and sobbed! Going into a large, strange school as a seventh grader was a bit daunting to me, knowing no one (except my brother, Ken). I went from being well-liked by many friends to being a nobody who ate lunch next to my brother. (None of the other girls ate next to the boys!)

Eventually I made a friend or two and survived. I did fairly well academically, graduating 13th out of 130 students, but always felt inferior due to my age. Sadly, being two years younger than many of my classmates also facilitated my falling into some of the many pitfalls common to adolescence.

I dated a young man in high school for nearly three years. He was a basketball player and his hero was Pete Maravich. We had some good times together, but I knew in my heart that

1 Cows, Chores, and Church

I would not marry him. Teen girls in the 1970s—myself included—were infused with the feminist ideals bursting on the scene, in the culture and in the schools. Stay-at-home motherhood was definitely not part of the plan, but careers and abortion surely were. I was steeped in this ideology; there was little rebuttal offered in school or at home.

Eager to begin the career path, I was able to gain employment at the local nursing home as a nurse's aide when I was 15. I went there after school and worked until 10 p.m. I loved caring for the elderly, though it was hard, back-breaking work. I guess I was used to hard work! This is where I encountered co-workers who smoked cigarettes…so naturally I took up smoking surreptitiously. My parents would have been appalled, to put it lightly, had they known. ("Mom, did you know?!")

I was growing up fast. In order to work, I needed transportation so I was able to purchase my first car at 16 with a loan from our local bank, co-signed by my father. The car was a 1968 Buick Skylark with 68,000 miles on it. One day the car was out of commission and I had to get to work. No one was home to drive me there, so I borrowed Randy's motorcycle. I had recently learned how to ride it and I thought I was being very resourceful as I gleefully sped away. My mother didn't share my glee and had someone drive a car to the nursing home and drop it off so I didn't ride the motorcycle home after work!

My Buick and I had quite an affair together for eight years. It took me many places, with or without friends. When my cousin was in an accident and in the hospital in Ann Arbor, I drove down to visit her. I drove to Indiana, to northern Michigan, and many places in between. The car finally came to its resting place back on the farm years after I had moved away and married.

I graduated from high school at 16 and went to Bethel College in Mishawaka, Indiana with Ken. We had been together throughout our years of schooling so it seemed natural to attend the same college together. This Christian school is affiliated with the Missionary Church which our family had been attending. I decided to major in music, so I enrolled in various music classes (including Music Theory, which I nearly failed), sang in two different choirs and played flute in the orchestra.

One of my most formative experiences at Bethel was singing in what was called the Oratorio Society. The main work of this choir was to perform Handel's *Messiah* every year. Exposure to this remarkable piece of music opened my mind again to the grandeur of God. (Fifteen years later I was privileged to join an adult choir which performed *Messiah* in a

1 Cows, Chores, and Church

town close to my home.) I still love to hum along every time I hear this piece of music.

Another unforgettable memory of my one year at Bethel College was the experience of singing in the concert choir. This group embarked on a choir tour every year, traveling throughout Indiana, Michigan, Ohio, Pennsylvania, and New York performing at various churches and colleges. For a small-town farm girl, this was really eye-opening! I reveled in the beautiful music, exquisite church architecture, historical colleges, and big cities! We spent some time in New York City. While there, several friends and I got lost and were separated from the rest of the choir. We had to find our way back through the dark New York subways at night...a frightful experience and not something I'd like to do again!

This year at Bethel College had another major impact on my life. As I began thinking more about the meaning of existence and asking the big questions ("Why am I here? What happens after this life?") I became disillusioned with Christianity as presented in this Protestant context. Rules for living seemed arbitrary and restrictive to me. Without making a decisive break with Christianity, I began to distance myself from faith in God. I was dating some young men at Bethel but I could not embrace their views of God and religion. I also began to question the wisdom of majoring in music. It seemed unlikely I would be able to make a career of it. At the end of my first year, I decided to return home and go back to work at the nursing home where I was previously employed.

Back home at 17, I immersed myself in working full-time, picking up more questionable habits from my co-workers. Christianity took a back seat. My independent nature led me to take an auto mechanics course so I could care for my Buick myself. My mother often tells the story of her waking up one morning after I had worked night shift and not seeing me asleep in my bed. She looked all over for me and found me in the garage, changing the spark plug wires in my car.

It's such a mystery how God works in our lives, even without our being aware of it. I don't remember being prayerful or attentive to God, but He was leading me on the path that would eventually bring me to Him. Working at the nursing home prompted me to consider nursing as a career. I talked to several of the nurses there, as well as a high school friend who had gone on to nursing school, and decided to apply at various schools.

While waiting to hear from nursing schools, a friend invited me to attend Michigan State University (MSU) with her for a quarter term (MSU's schedule at the time) in the spring of 1976. I saw it as another adventure, so signed up for some general education classes and choir. One class was *The New Testament as Literature*. I'm not sure why I chose that class. I met a fellow there who became a dear friend and who

1   Cows, Chores, and Church

later was the pianist at my wedding. His name was Tom and he had a friend, Steve, who had aspirations of becoming a preacher. He led Bible studies which I attended; faith began to grow. Steve convinced me that I needed to be baptized again and that I should speak in tongues. Years later, I learned that one cannot be baptized a second time.

> Incorporated into Christ by Baptism, the person baptized is configured to Christ. Baptism seals the Christian with the indelible spiritual mark (*character*) of his belonging to Christ. No sin can erase this mark, even if sin prevents Baptism from bearing the fruits of salvation. Given once for all, Baptism cannot be repeated.[6]

I didn't know this at the time however, so we dutifully went down to the Red Cedar River on MSU's campus and I was "re-baptized"; I did not speak in tongues, which led me to once again become skeptical of the whole religion idea.

Several nursing schools accepted me and I chose Butterworth Hospital School of Nursing in Grand Rapids, Michigan. (The nursing school no longer exists and the hospital later changed its name to Spectrum Health.) I had

---

[6] *Catechism of the Catholic Church*, par. 1272.

painstakingly listed the pros and cons of all the schools, but when it came right down to choosing, I went with my intuition. God again led me unknowingly, as this decision laid the groundwork for a major step forward on the path to Jesus Christ and His Church.

2
Courtship with a Catholic?!

August 26, 1976—a date I will never forget. My parents dropped me off at the student nurses' residence. I was unaware of the intense educational experience I was about to begin, but sharing it with three roommates lessened the shock. One of these girls, Pam, became a life-long friend, sharing the joys and trials of many years.

At the ripe old age of 18, I had decided, upon entering nursing school, to eschew looking for a boyfriend or husband. I didn't have a clear sense of who I was or what I believed, but I determined to make a way for myself with a nursing career. The nursing students spent their first year at the local junior college taking basic courses in sciences and liberal arts. One of our classes was Psychology 101. My roommates and I arrived at the classroom and sat next to each other in the second row. Three young men sat in the front row. This was unusual, as most of the nursing classes were filled with young ladies.

One day I noticed that one of the men had hiking boots on and they were dripping slush on the floor. The next day this same fellow had moved back one row into my seat! So my friends and I split up and sat on either side of him. I was to his right. I learned that his name was Edward Stuart. We would sometimes comment on the teacher or the class content to each other. He was studying pre-med, was ten years older than me—he was 28—and Catholic. I was intrigued by his thoughtful remarks and his sincerity. He didn't speak superficially about inane things, but deeply about meaningful things. Psychology class gave us plenty to ponder; I remember learning about and discussing Dr. Elizabeth Kubler-Ross' *Five Stages of Grief.* Talking about death is probably not the most common topic of discussion among young adults. Soon our conversations continued while walking together to our next classes.

Not long after that, I shared with my roommates that he was the type of man I could marry. One day in December, I found a package in my mailbox at the nurses' residence, wrapped in Christmas paper. The tag said "To Miss F. Hampshire, From E.S." I excitedly rushed to my room and showed it to my roommates as we tried to figure out who E.S. was. Pam shouted out, "It's Ed Stuart!" The package contained two 8" x 10" pictures of Alaska which he had taken when he lived there. (One was of the Brooks Range mountains, which he loved, and the other was a time elapsed photo of the sun rising and setting during one of the shortest days of the year.) The card with the package said, "Hope you like the pictures. Have a nice Christmas. Hope to see you next semester." I was over the top happy!

He called me to ask for a date soon afterwards, during Christmas vacation. (Few of the nursing students traveled home during holiday vacations.) My roommates were all excited and helped me get dolled up, with curled hair and makeup. We either went to a movie or to the symphony; I can't remember which. Frequent dates followed; we drove to Lake Michigan often, and he enjoyed taking me to visit his grandmother in Tustin, a small town in northern Michigan. Traveling to these places allowed us to have extended conversations as we slowly began to fall in love.

His Catholic faith gave us much to discuss. As may have been apparent, I grew up in a rather biased, anti-Catholic environment. Several families in our farming community were Catholic but did not seem to be authentic witnesses to faith in God. Rumors of alcoholic Catholic priests permeated the air. Now Ed and I began two years of dialogue and arguments about the Christian faith.

I didn't set out to study Catholicism. I really didn't want anything to do with it, as I was still in my rebellious phase. But I did admire Ed's faith and his intelligence. I had encountered intellectual people who scoffed at Christianity, but very few who embraced it with such tenacity as Ed did.

In our time together we talked, and when we were apart we wrote letters to each other. I have kept many of his letters to me. In February of the next year, 1977, I shared with him a letter I received from one of those intellectual friends who was flirting with philosophies contrary to Christianity; in this particular letter, he was denigrating marriage, claiming it was an obstacle to personal growth. I was very interested to see what Ed Stuart had to say about it!

Here is his response. But first, a taste of his humor.

Well, here is another one [letter]. *I've just had my Saturday night bubble bath and packed some art history into my cortical neurons and am about to eat my daily orange…if you see any water stains on this paper, it's not from me drooling but from my orange.*

Keep in mind that he is writing to a person who is not particularly "religious" (me) as you read how he addresses whether or not marriage is a hindrance to personal growth.

Growth must be defined before any reasonable argument can be constructed. Growth may mean accumulation of a collage of varied experiences in an effort to see and feel all that life has to offer. I would define growth as refining one's knowledge of himself and others by establishing meaningful interpersonal relationships in which each gives the best he has (often at a sacrifice) to the others. Growth is the process of integrating the components of life into a unified structure—or of balancing the emotional, rational and religious attributes inherent in man. Growth is expanding one's perspective of how others feel and developing the patience to understand them even when their behavior is less than ideal, for all men are under stress and have suffered.

After several more paragraphs, he concluded with a poem by Stephen Grellet, which he said he found on a Christmas card.

I shall pass through this world but once.
If therefore, there be any kindness I can show,
Or any good I can do,
Let me do it now;
Let me not defer it or neglect it,
For I shall not pass this way again.

My mother had often told me as a young girl to marry someone smarter than myself. Maybe unconsciously I was looking for that man smarter than me…now I believed I had found him. I knew it with certainty some time later when I read a paper he wrote for a class. The topic was euthanasia. I had never heard the word and didn't know what it was! His paper gave a thorough and logical rebuttal to the proponents of this increasingly common immoral practice. His thoughtful critique was based on the moral principles of the Catholic Church, though he was not explicit about it, and I did not appreciate that at the time. Catholicism to me was still a strange mystery religion!

Early in the summer of 1977 I moved back home to work on the farm milking cows until nursing school began again in August. This next letter from Ed is dated June 15. On the second page he tells me that he is planning to take a few weeks off about September 1 and go to Alaska. (He was stationed at the Army base, Ft. Greely, in Delta Junction, Alaska in the early 70s, and lived there as a civilian just before meeting me at the junior college.)

> *If I do some hitchhiking, I think I could get there quite cheap. Once I get there, I can live very cheap with people I know. It's the nicest time of year up there and I could help out with the grain harvest.*

My heart sang! A city boy who loves the farm life! The next page was a real zinger though.

2 Courtship With a Catholic?!

We have gone together long enough to at least consider marriage.

My thoughts were racing at this point. What will he say? We must have been discussing the general topic of marriage and other aspects of Christianity because then he writes,

I know what [St.] Paul says—but like I said, Paul was not omniscient (only God is) and didn't know how long it would be until the end of the world. I think Paul was kind of down on women—but that's his problem.

*The Bible is a chronicle of: the spiritual development of the Jews, the coming of Christ, and the days of the early Church. It is not a sociology book or science text. It doesn't tell us how to cure diseases through medicine—but does that mean we shouldn't try? The greatest commandment was not to read Scriptures—but to **love God** and **one another.** Scriptures can give many valuable insights. But reading is one thing and doing is another. Many so-called religious people are spiritual bookworms instead of practitioners. One person who encourages the down-trodden or feeds the hungry or forgives another is worth ten Bible-toting and quoting horses' asses. The Pharisees were the Bible quoters of Jesus'*

> time. Please don't think that I think quoting the Bible is wrong—but if it is **all** a person does, he is no better than a Pharisee. If we don't agree on that, at least, then we are miles apart on religion.

These extensive quotes from Ed's letters illustrate the level of discussions we were having, questions that two people should be considering before marriage, as well as the particular difficulties that arise when two different belief systems come together. Later in this same letter, he says:

> I guess I should consider children as a topic. Please bear with me. I hope I don't sound dogmatic or critical—I just want to point up the realities of the situation. I would want children. I believe they are a very important part of marriage and life rather than "mistakes" to be tolerated. If we couldn't have kids, I, personally, would like to adopt, but it would, of course, be our decision, i.e., a joint decision. I doubt if I could justify **my own** use of birth control—but it would be, of course, your option with regard to yourself.
>
> Again, religion rears its head. I doubt if I would ever change religions. I also doubt I would give up religion altogether. I doubt you are as pinned to your

religion as I am to mine. In my belief, the best environment for raising children is one in which there is religious unity—but I really doubt you would ever consider becoming Catholic. That sort of thing is too much to ask.

I remember you said that you wouldn't want to teach your children anything you didn't believe in—but I guess I feel the same way. What would we do then? Could we raise them under both religions? Would such a thing even be possible? Religious denomination just shouldn't matter that much, but it is idealistic to believe it doesn't matter at all. With regard to ourselves, I would say that I would go into ecstasy if you joined my religion, but if you didn't, I would hope that you would at least want to learn the truth about it—maybe in a class, and would go to church with me as I would with you if you wanted me to. What would happen to our children, I don't know. Can you think of a compromise? Think how easy it would be to marry a Protestant farm boy who was your own age. [Ed was 29 and I was 19 when this letter was written.]

Love can surmount all this. Do we love each other enough? I love you, but do I know love well enough to know if it is strong enough? Do you really love me—

> *that is, enough to put up with my weaknesses and faults, enough to put me above your family in the sense that your identity as Fae Stuart would be at least as important to you as your identity as Fae Hampshire?*

Critical questions, questions that many couples grapple with when considering marriage. What a leap of faith it can be, to pledge oneself totally to another person. I was beginning to think that I could answer yes, yes, and yes to his important questions.

The topic of Ed's next letter, dated June 28, 1977, was our different ideas about church attendance.

> *I sort of felt bad when you didn't want me to go to church. It kind of put me on the spot. That's one of those things you would have to put up with. I guess I know how you feel about "religion" (what it often is) vs religion (what it can be). I myself often get disgusted with the service or the distractions but that's mostly due to my impatience. I try to remember that the church is only as good as its members. So I try to gut it out and give it a chance and hopefully do something to make it better. I almost feel we would be closer on religion if you were a practicing Methodist*

rather than in your present state. [I was still skeptical of God's existence and disdained what I perceived to be religious hypocrisy.]

I know what you are going through. I went through it. Most thinking people do. All I can say is that in many ways you are right—the only thing is that men and organizations are not perfect and never will be. If we look for an excuse not to go to church we can find it very easily. We shouldn't go against the Master because we have a squabble with one of his servants. No man is a spiritual island.

Again I should say that I guess I would never give up religion—and if that really bugs you like I think it might, maybe we should seriously question the real depth of our relationship. Please send a letter and discuss this. [Neither of us had access to a telephone, and even if we did, we both shared our deepest thoughts more fully in writing.]

I must have lightened up in my objections to religion and started asking more specific questions when I responded to the previous letter, as in mid-July he began to focus on differences between Protestantism and Catholicism rather than on the more general question of religion vs no religion.

2 Courtship With a Catholic?!

What don't Catholics agree with about Protestants? It depends on the Catholic and the Protestant. Last week a nice young [Protestant denomination] *person called me a "Pope-worshipping ass" right to my face. Obviously, this was a Christian in name only. I will admit that I have never met a Catholic who put down a Protestant (some must exist, but I've never met one), but I have met a lot of Protestants who put down Catholics. But, as above, most of these were Christians in name only. Parents tend to pass on evil feelings and intolerance and many kids lap it right up. The KKK (Ku Klux Klan) = Kikes (Jews), Koons (Blacks), and Katholics (me). The kind of intolerance represented by such as the KKK is incompatible with any type of Christianity and therefore doesn't involve a disagreement between Catholics and Protestants because Protestants are Christians.*

There are so many types of Protestants that one can't generalize on any points of disagreement. I can speak for no one but myself. A good Protestant who has found Christ and proves it by living like Christ is worth ten Catholics who only go through the motions of honoring God—and vice versa. **Being a Christian transcends denominations** *(but is not completely independent of them, for they represent Christ's*

46

Church). I disagree with any Protestant who thinks he alone is able to be saved and go to heaven, i.e., "only by being a _____ can you get to see God." Catholics have never believed that—some Protestant sects do. Catholics believe non-Christians are able to see God if [through no fault of their own,] they [have not heard the gospel and] live good and just lives.

I don't believe salvation is an instantaneous process consisting only of an emotional and intellectual outburst. Many, if not most Protestants, don't believe this, but some do. Salvation is a lifelong process of spiritual growth. I'm not saying that people can't have significant and lasting reorientations toward God—a change that can last a lifetime—but it is dangerous to believe that this change itself constitutes salvation. A "perfect" change and reorientation would, in effect, constitute salvation—but "Let he who is without sin...." I'm not perfect; is anyone?

As far as faith and works go, I don't see a problem at all even though these are the classic points of disagreement only because Luther separated them and focused on faith alone as the key to heaven. Faith and works can't be separated. Faith is essential for it is by belief that we acquire motivation to do works.

> Works are essential because Christ said they were. Please read Matthew 25—the whole thing. Faith alone is like an empty lamp or a buried treasure. In verses 45 and 46 Christ says, "In as much as ye did it not to one of the least of these, ye did it not to me. And these shall go into everlasting punishment...," i.e., Do or Die—pretty clear, I guess.
>
> Each of us at any one time is in a state, hopefully, of advancement toward God. Many are in retrogress, but we all can be ultimately forgiven and saved if we merely **will** it to happen by **accepting** Christ <u>and living</u> as he told us to. Active faith (vs passive faith) implies both **Belief** and **Actions**.

A love letter wouldn't be complete without some words of love. He concludes this letter with what, for me, was the essence of romantic love.

> I love you—what is it I love? At first it was parts of you—a smile, your face—then it was what you did, what you said; now it is just you as a person, not your attributes or components, but your existence.
> Love, Ed

2 Courtship With a Catholic?!

The day he sent that letter, I was writing to him. This is the only letter I have that I sent to him...maybe it's a guy thing not to save letters! While I was home for the summer I was living by myself in an empty house my brother, Randy, owned. This is part of my letter to Ed.

I walked into my bathroom today with bare feet and yucckk; the rugs were all wet. So I looked and looked and found the pipe from the sink wrapped with adhesive tape dripping like mad. Can you believe that? Wrapped with tape, now I've seen everything. I figure that's why they had the drain stopped up with a wad of paper towel! I guess I'll have to figure out how to fix that.

Tomorrow morning I am starting to work up [with a tractor and implement] *those 50 acres again. I'll be surprised if it doesn't need going over this time and once more at least. It was a mess. It sure is gonna be a hot job!*

Tonight just before I started milking I read a story in the Reader's Digest. As the sad ones always do, it got me all teary, but it was neat, it made me think some. I usually think pretty well while I'm milking. I wish you had been there so I could've shared with you. It seems I can tell you what I'm thinking, and you understand and know what I mean. And most importantly, you don't make me feel funny or ashamed for thinking things I do. I love that in you. Anyway, it was about a lady with cancer and I started thinking again about death and how close we all are to it all the time. Like you said, I think we need a "reminder" (a cemetery?) **often** of death. And I thought about all the things I want to do, what I want to be to other people and to myself before I die—and I thought about you and all you've done and what you want to do, wondered what you want—and it hit me that we are both so close to death, you know?

==I want to live so that it's not all a waste; I want to live to do things for and be things to others so a part of me will go beyond my death.== I really want to help people, you know—not so much to help them with any big things (which I'd be incapable of anyway) but maybe to just make someone happy for a few minutes, or encourage a smile, or after I'm a nurse to make someone more physically comfortable. I want to share my life with someone who appreciates the things I do so that we can enjoy them together. I want to go through hard times together so we can work together. I don't know, when I think of all these things (not often enough) I get so sad, so frustrated, because it seems I *will never fulfill what I really want my life to be. And I may get killed tomorrow and then what?*

I love you very much, Edward. I hope neither of us dies until we can share a bit more of ourselves with each other. It's getting dark and I can't see. Miss you.

Love, Fae

The last courtship letter I have from Ed seems to point towards marriage, but typically for him, indecision looms large.

Sometimes I think I'd like to be married. If I had some kind of a job I liked and had stability I probably would. You'll have to be mighty patient to wait for me to straighten out. If you were smart you would leave me now. The most important thing is that you finish your nursing [school].

I think we get along well. We've sort of reached a stalemate on religion, but I think you're big enough to accept my own commitment and I'm sure I understand your position pretty well after all that we have talked. I don't think we would try to interfere with each other yet hopefully we could share each other's company at church occasionally.

2 Courtship With a Catholic?!

I love you and always will no matter what happens. You are the love of my life and I will never forget you. With deep love, Ed

By this time I was pretty sure I wanted to marry him! He needed a bit of encouragement so one day I said, "Well, we might as well get married." He must have agreed for during Christmas break that year, 1977, we bought a ring at a jewelry store in downtown Grand Rapids. Typically, Ed didn't say we were going to the store to buy an engagement ring; we just looked around and I found a ring I really liked and asked if we could buy it. It happened to have a small diamond in it, so it sufficed for an engagement ring! Ed did come around though—on a cold, sunny day in January 1978, on the shore of Lake Michigan—he knelt down and asked me to marry him.

3
Surprised by the Spirit

Ed registered us for a Pre-Cana weekend, a program of marriage preparation required by the Catholic Church. One of the presentations was on something called natural family planning (the common terminology then; today it is also known as fertility awareness); by a priest, no less. This did not go well. I sat through it, muttering under my breath how ridiculous this was and that this man didn't know what he was talking about. *I* knew all about the latest scientific methods of controlling birth. In the Obstetrics/Gynecology portion of my education we were trained in the current methods of birth control. We learned how to "educate" women upon their release from the hospital after delivering a baby. This all seemed right and good to me. I proclaimed to Ed that this "NFP" stuff was just the same as artificial means, that the goal for both methods is the same—avoiding pregnancy. Ed did not answer me; he may have thought it was useless to try to explain, but God took note of my prideful outburst and gently opened my eyes to the truth not so many years later.

All the while, Ed was probably wondering how best to introduce me to the Catholic Mass. He understood I had never experienced formal liturgy, so before he invited me to attend

Mass, he took me to a Lutheran service to introduce it in a Protestant context. I was still mystified, and it felt very unfamiliar to me. It did however, lessen the shock when I did attend Mass for the first time. I didn't know anything about the Mass as the re-presentation of Jesus' sacrifice on the cross, but I will never forget how I felt seeing Ed *kneel*. The impact of this act of humility was profound. I had never experienced anything like it, and I marveled at whatever or Whomever it was that elicited this reverence.

Nevertheless, I informed Ed that I would not become Catholic. (This bold statement reminds me of the proclamation to my nursing school roommates that I could never marry a doctor or a Catholic! I proceeded to get engaged to a Catholic pre-med student.) Ed asked me to at least take a class so I could understand his religion better. I agreed, and argued my way through what is called an RCIA class (Rite of Christian Initiation for Adults) at the Catholic Information Center in Grand Rapids.

Breaking the news of our engagement to my parents wasn't the easiest thing, but they did not voice their displeasure too much. In their eyes, Ed definitely had some strikes against him as my future husband. He was a city boy, much older, and, worst of all, he was Catholic. My maternal grandmother asked me, "Couldn't you find yourself a nice Protestant boy?!" But my family did begin the necessary preparations for a wedding, which, true to my nature, was a bit out of the ordinary.

Ed, being Catholic, needed to follow the form of a Catholic wedding in order for our marriage to be valid. I did not feel at all bound by this—which was why I insisted on getting married in Grandma Alice's front yard. I didn't feel bound by the stipulation that I agree to raise any children we may have in the Catholic faith either. When Ed and I went to see his priest about marriage, I was asked if I promised to raise the children as Catholics. This took me by surprise—and I promptly said, "No!" Ed and the priest looked at each other in dead silence, then the priest said to Ed, "Do *you* promise to raise the children as Catholics?" He assured the priest that he would. I didn't know it at the time, because I had no understanding of how the Church handles mixed marriages, but the priest asked for and received from the bishop the necessary permissions, or dispensations, for Ed not only to marry a non-Catholic, but to marry outside of a Catholic church with a Protestant minister attending. Many years later I wondered about the validity of our marriage because I didn't know the dispensations had been granted. I contacted Ed's parish and was able to see the records which assured me that, yes, our marriage was valid. That was a relief!

3   Surprised by the Spirit

Wedding preparations were underway and my family worked hard to make it a memorable day for us. I was so thankful for their expressions of love through the work of their hands. My mother had beautiful penmanship, so I asked her to handwrite the invitations on flowered paper I purchased. She did such a lovely job, keepsake-worthy! Grandma Alice was working in her flower beds to make sure they would look perfect for the June 3 wedding in her front yard; my father and brothers were planning how to get the chores all done before the evening wedding and bring the upright piano from my parents' home to Grandma Alice's yard; and my aunt agreed to arrange fresh flowers for my bouquet. The reception was to be at my parents' home with a homemade meal, so my mother and grandmothers were very busy planning the dishes I had requested. I decided to have no bridesmaids or groomsmen or ushers for the wedding ... I liked simplicity and that seemed like a complication. My brother Ken was preparing to sing *The Prayer of St. Francis* (Ed chose this song) accompanied by my MSU friend, Tom, on the piano. I practiced a song to sing for Ed, and he prepared a Scripture reading. The young pastor who witnessed our marriage was from the same Lamotte Missionary Church that I had attended with my family. Ours was the first marriage he was to witness.

3   *Surprised by the Spirit*

An incident occurred a couple of weeks before the wedding. I had driven my father somewhere. Upon our return to my grandparents' home, I pulled into their driveway and drove around to the back of the house. I shut off the ignition and my father seemed to want to say something. Finally, he said, "We have decided that this is not the man for you to marry. He is ten years older than you, and men typically die seven years sooner than women, which means you could have seventeen years alone." In my shock I could not think of any arguments or any questions, but I knew in the deepest part of me what I would answer. I quietly said, "I *am* going to marry him," and got out of the truck. I know my parents truly thought it best for me not to marry Ed, and I harbored no resentment against them. God gave me the grace to stay true to my love for Ed and my vocation to marriage with him, which was one of the most important decisions I was to make in my life.

June 3 arrived, cool and sunny. Rain was in the forecast; we did have Plan B, to move the wedding to the Missionary Church if necessary. Sure enough, rain fell off and on through the day. But about an hour before the wedding, the clouds scattered and the sun peeked out. The grass and leaves sparkled like diamonds as the chairs were toweled off and the piano uncovered. Cows grazed contentedly in the pasture nearby. The ceremony began with the pastor's prayer in thanksgiving for the break in the rain. Our wedding was very "nonCatholic," in the sense that Ed and I planned the order of service and wrote our own vows (which was trendy in those days). Ed had written opening remarks, sounding very much like the scientific man that he was, with words like atoms, molecules, and living tissue. I think the wedding guests were chuckling, saying, "Yep, that sure sounds like Ed alright!" The pastor spoke of the commitment and permanence of marriage after Ed and I had spoken our vows. What I remember most vividly about our wedding is the closing prayer. The last few lines of this prayer remained in my memory through all of our marriage, long after I had forgotten many elements of the wedding. The pastor prayed:

> *God of love, you have established marriage for the welfare and happiness of us, mankind. The plan originated with You, and only with You can we work it out with joy.*
>
> *I pray that you would bless this husband, Ed. Bless him as leader and provider of their home. Strengthen him in all the pressures of life. And may his strength be Fae's protection, his character her boast and her pride, and may he so live that she will find in him the haven that the heart of a woman truly longs for.*

Bless Fae, this loving wife, give her a tenderness that will make her great, a deep sense of understanding, and a great faith in You. Give her that inner beauty of the soul that never fades, and that eternal youth that is found holding tightly to things that never age and grow old.

Teach them that marriage is not living merely for each other, it is two uniting and joining hands to serve You. **Give them a great spiritual purpose in life.** *May they seek first the kingdom of God and His righteousness and the other things shall be added to them.*

May they not expect that perfection of each other that belongs only to You. May they minimize each other's weaknesses, be swift to praise and magnify each other's points of strength, and see each other through a lover's kind and patient eyes.

Give them enough tears to keep them tender, enough hurts to keep them humane, enough of failure to keep their hands clenched tightly in Yours, and enough success to make them sure they walk with God.

When life is done, and the sun is setting, may they be found then as now, still hand in hand, still thanking You for each other; may they serve You

happily, faithfully, together, until at last, one shall lay the other into the arms of God.
This we ask together, great Lover of our souls. Amen.

It took me by surprise, as I wasn't expecting to be reminded of death at my wedding. The fact that one of us would likely be alone one day was so incongruous as we pledged ourselves to each other in fidelity that it nearly took my breath away. And what did the pastor mean when he prayed that Ed and I would have a great spiritual purpose in life? We surely didn't see anything like that in our future.

After a delicious reception meal lovingly prepared by my family, Ed and I headed off on our honeymoon to Alaska, his favorite place. He was eager to introduce me to his friends and to share the beauty of that wild place with me. We flew from Grand Rapids to Seattle, spent a couple of days there, then flew to Fairbanks. His elderly friend, Randy (who had fought at Normandy on D-Day) picked us up and welcomed us to his simple home. We stayed with Randy and with other friends, Carol and Jon, Ed's former boss, for 2 ½ weeks, visiting and sightseeing.

We started our trip home on a bus from Delta Junction to Whitehorse, Yukon. From there we enjoyed a breathtaking ride on the White Pass and Yukon Route railway, completed in

1900, to Skagway, Alaska and caught the Alaskan ferry boat. One of the boat's stops was at Sitka. We disembarked and visited the beautiful Russian Orthodox Cathedral. The abundant artwork and precious items in this church pricked my Protestant feelings and I let loose with the tired canard, "If the Catholic Church sold all their treasures, they could help the poor." (The difference between the Catholic Church and the Orthodox Church was lost on me.) Dear Ed...he must have sighed, then patiently tried to explain that the Church keeps these treasures so all people can appreciate them, rather than merely the few people who might keep them in their private homes. He probably also pointed out that the Catholic Church is one of the leading institutions to serve the poor around the world. So I sulked for a while, but I couldn't stay upset for long...we were on our honeymoon! The ferry boat eventually docked in Prince Rupert, British Columbia and we got on a Canadian National train heading east. After a one-night stop in beautiful Jasper, Alberta we traveled to Sault Ste. Marie, Ontario where Ed's mother picked us up. It was an unforgettable month-long trip.

 Now decisions needed to be made. Ed had been accepted at all three Michigan medical schools and I still had one more year of nursing school. If he decided to go to med school, we would have to live apart from one another. If he decided not to go to med school, what would he do? (He did have a master's

8 Surprised by the Spirit

degree in electrical engineering.) If he decided to go to school, which one should he choose? I tried not to influence his decision, but I think he suspected I wasn't that enthusiastic about being married to a doctor. I'm sure he must have prayed about this decision, and he eventually joined the class at the University of Michigan medical school for the fall of 1978.

Ed and I thus began our married life with him in his first year of medical school in Ann Arbor and me in my final year of nursing school in Grand Rapids. I rented a small, third-floor apartment in a historic neighborhood not far from Butterworth Hospital, and he stayed in a student dorm at the university. We traveled back and forth on weekends when our homework wasn't too demanding.

1978 was to be a momentous year in the Catholic Church as well as in my own life, when the Holy Spirit performed mighty works. Just as the events in the Church of that year were surprising and unexpected, with the election of two popes, so were the events in my life. Ed and I had come to an understanding of each other's faith to the extent that there was a certain peace between us. When Pope Paul VI died and the Cardinals' conclave met to elect the next Pope, Ed asked me to watch it on TV so I could tell him about it. He had no way to watch it where he lived, but we had received a tiny, black and white TV from his grandfather and it was set up in my little apartment. As should be clear by now, I had no intention of becoming Catholic and Ed had accepted this. On August 26, 1978—exactly two years from the day I arrived at nursing school—as I watched all the pomp and circumstance, the formality, the vestments, the bishops and cardinals surrounding Pope John Paul I's election, I couldn't understand "what all the fuss was about. Why is this such a big deal?" I was clueless and even perturbed. What happened next can be explained only by the power of the Holy Spirit. In that moment, this thought entered my mind: "I could become Catholic and surprise Ed!" It was like a light switch had gone on; one second I was in the dark, the next second I was bathed in light. Peace came over me and I was almost giddy with anticipation at becoming Catholic!

I don't remember Ed's reaction when I told him. He most assuredly would have been surprised, maybe even skeptical, but I followed through with this inspiration. Ed inquired with the Catholic Information Center where I had attended RCIA and I was given permission to enter the Church as soon as possible. In a private ceremony on September 16, 1978 I made a solemn profession of faith in the Roman Catholic Church and received my first Holy Communion and Confirmation. I marveled at the fact that my parents traveled four hours to be there with me. They didn't tell me until many years later that they believed so strongly in the importance of unity in marriage that they overlooked the fact that it was Catholicism that united us!

How did this radical conversion of heart come about? I pondered this question for years, and one day I heard this story: Fr. John Riccardo, a well-known Catholic priest and evangelist, related that his mother said with great emotion to her husband as he lay in the casket at his funeral, "I know Christ because of you." That was it—the foundation of my own radical conversion. My heart was open to hear the Holy Spirit and to respond, to desire to know Christ, from Ed's example of a faithful life and his lucid explanations of Christianity and Catholicism. While I had investigated and studied Church teaching, my conversion was not based on this study but simply an answer to God's call. "O chosen people, proclaim the mighty works of Him who called you out of darkness into His wonderful light!"[7] "For by grace you have been saved through faith, and this is not from you; it is the gift from God..." (Ephesians 2:8). Faith had always been a struggle for me, because I wanted to figure things out, to understand. God had renewed this spark of faith through Ed, but I had yet to learn that understanding does not precede faith, but faith precedes understanding.

---

[7] Entrance Antiphon, Monday of 27th week in Ordinary Time.

3 Surprised by the Spirit

The fallout from the "Great Confusion" of the 1970s in the American Church resulted in the fact that I was not taught about the necessity of confessing my sins in the sacrament of Confession before receiving my first Holy Communion. Thus, it was nearly three years later that I first went to Confession! Fear and pride and lack of understanding (receiving the Body, Blood, Soul, and Divinity of Jesus in Holy Communion without ever going to Confession is a serious matter), all played a part in my delay in receiving the gracious mercy of God in Confession.

Oh, and Mary, our Blessed Mother! I remember as a child discovering Gounod's *Ave Maria* in my mother's Scribner's Radio Music Library, a nine-volume set of piano music. It is so beautiful, but I was told, "We don't play that song." I was sad and didn't understand why I couldn't play it, but I simply accepted that Mary was someone dark, mysterious, to keep hidden or to ignore. I don't recall ever hearing her name mentioned at our Protestant church—maybe at Christmas. So my love for the Blessed Virgin Mary took years to grow, bit by bit.

It started out on rocky ground. I was at a diocesan retreat, the first one I ever attended. Everyone else was praying the rosary the first evening. I finally figured out where they were, as I could hear them in the chapel. I stopped outside the door and listened. They were repeating this Hail Mary prayer over

8 Surprised by the Spirit

and over! I was mortified, and turned around and went to my room, thinking, "What have I gotten myself into?" I think our Blessed Mother was smiling as She just poured out graces and love on me, as this retreat was the place I finally realized I needed to go to Confession! No one had taught me the procedure, so the priest must have been amused at my clumsy attempts to admit my sins.

I also had difficulty accepting the efficacy of the sacrament of Baptism. In my understanding, the Missionary Church I had attended as a teenager believed that Baptism was merely a sign that one had accepted Jesus Christ as Lord and Savior. The Catholic Church believes and teaches very clearly about sanctifying grace which God infuses into the soul at Baptism, without which it is not ordinarily possible to enter the kingdom of God (John 3:5). It took me years to assent to this in my heart, and Ed and I discussed it vigorously. Our first three children were not baptized until I had worked through this dilemma when they were ages 5, 2, and 1.

The Real Presence of Jesus in the Holy Eucharist however, made perfect sense to me. John 6 could not be any clearer. Verse 35 reads, "Jesus said to them, 'I am the bread of life; whoever comes to me will never hunger, and whoever believes in me will never thirst.' " In verses 51-53, Jesus is even more emphatic: " 'I am the living bread that came down from heaven; whoever eats this bread will live forever; and the bread that I will give is my flesh for the life of the world.'

"The Jews quarreled among themselves, saying, 'How can this man give us his flesh to eat?'

"Jesus said to them, 'Amen, amen, I say to you, unless you eat the flesh of the Son of Man and drink his blood, you do not have life within you.' " If God can become a tiny baby, He can surely turn bread and wine into Jesus' Body and Blood. It was so joyous the first time that Ed and I received Jesus into our souls together!

Though we were finally united in faith, there would always be a difference between us. I read a short article by Patti Defilippis in 1998, twenty years after I converted to Catholicism. It appeared in the newsletter of St. Luke Productions. She was a convert too, and she wrote:

> *This* [Catholic] *faith is not part of my native culture. When I immerse myself in the trappings of the Church, I can only feel comfortable so long, and then I begin to feel like a stranger in a strange land. I find this Catholic "country" beautiful and profoundly moving, but I will always be an immigrant. This is not true for my husband or children, who have lived all their lives in a Catholic world. Perhaps this feeling is only something a convert can understand.*

Twenty years after my conversion, I wrote in the margin of the newsletter, "I understand." Yet I felt a wonderful sense of freedom in the Catholic Church! It was the seemingly arbitrary rules and what I saw as the superficiality of Protestantism which had instigated my exodus out of Christianity. Now I found reason along with faith. Now the Catholic Church's teaching offered a depth I had not known before. My desire for understanding found untold riches to explore!

After this momentous change in our lives, we both finished up the academic year and finally, June 1979 meant graduation from nursing school—oh, joy!—and reunion with my husband—double joy!!

4
Faith and Fertility

After a camping trip to the Rocky Mountains in Colorado that summer, Ed and I moved into married housing on the north end of the University of Michigan's campus. We chose a two-bedroom apartment, as we learned that I was unexpectedly pregnant! With my newly-acquired medical knowledge, I had convinced myself that I would probably not ever conceive a child naturally...so naturally, God showed us He is the Giver of all Life. While filled with wonder at this miracle, I was somewhat ambivalent. I had just become an RN, gotten a job at Mott Children's Hospital in Ann Arbor, and was now nauseated beyond anything I'd ever felt before. Definitely not part of my career plan.

Then came the day of the first ultrasound and everything changed. I could not believe what I was seeing on the screen—a beautifully-formed child—our own child! My heart melted and any ambivalence vanished. The first step toward dismantling my acceptance of abortion was taken. (In high school I wrote a clinical research paper on the topic, describing the various methods with no sense of hesitation or revulsion. I had imbibed the spirit of the age.) God knew that I could only take one small step at a time toward Him. The next step, which finally pushed me off the fence about abortion, came when I read a book some years later by Dr. John Wilke, *Handbook on Abortion*. Filled with photos of actual aborted children, I was horrified. I can remember exactly where I was when I saw these pictures and thought, *How can this be legal?! How could anyone do this*? Suddenly I was pro-life, and this became an unalterable part of my deepest being.

Ed and I settled into a routine of school and work. Anyone who is familiar with medical school knows that it is an all-consuming experience of study and immersion in the medical world. I thought nursing school was intense…Ed's experience was much more so. When he was home, he was studying, though we did try to discuss our days, sharing an understanding of the medical/nursing worlds. I enjoyed my job on the Arthritis and Plastic Surgery unit at the hospital (the only adult floor in the children's hospital at the time). I cared for individuals with autoimmune diseases, those undergoing cosmetic plastic surgery, and paraplegic and quadriplegic patients undergoing reparative wound surgeries. I worked until a few weeks before my baby's due date, then waited impatiently!

As first-time parents, we went to the hospital too early when labor began. Home again, we were lying on our bed watching the 11 o'clock news when my water broke. This first experience of labor pains was a bit of a shock, to say the least.

4   *Faith and Fertility*

Off we went again to the hospital. I don't remember the sequence of events too clearly, as in those days—1980—I was given Demerol for the pain. This made me sleepy and I would awaken with a jerk when each contraction began. Progress was slow, so an x-ray was ordered...again, this was 1980! (When a British physician and epidemiologist, Alice Stewart, raised an alarm in 1956 about the use of x-rays during pregnancy due to a higher incidence of childhood cancers, she was attacked by medical establishments both in Britain and the U.S. It took twenty-five years before Stewart's findings were acknowledged and the practice of x-raying pregnant women was abandoned.)[8] The report came back that my sacrum was flat rather than having a nice normal curve; therefore, it was determined that I would not be able to deliver the baby vaginally but would need a Caesarean section (C-section). I was a bit alarmed, having observed C-sections in nursing school, but by this time, a day and a half after labor had begun, I was ready to submit to the knife.

Ed and I couldn't agree on what to name the baby, either boy or girl. So we compromised; if the baby was a boy, Ed would choose the first name and I the middle name. If the baby was a girl, I would choose the first name and he the

---

[8] Dr. Judy Mikovits and Kent Heckenlively, J.D., *Plague of Corruption: Restoring Faith in the Promise of Science* (New York: Skyhorse Publishing, 2020), xv.

71

middle name. As we discovered Baby Stuart to be a boy, Ed chose the name Joseph for St. Joseph, and I chose Todd, just because I liked it. I asked though, that we always call our son Joseph, not a nickname. If the baby had been a girl, the name would have been Katie.

This was now Ed's second year in medical school. Along with learning to nurture a newborn, we got involved with a volunteer effort to provide medical care and assistance to Vietnamese refugees. This was the era of the "Boat People," those who fled Vietnam by boat or ship following the end of the Vietnam War in 1975. This migration peaked in 1978 and 1979, and by 1980, the United States was accepting and resettling these brave people. Ed and I were in charge of procuring the medical care for a family of four and a single adult man. What a wonderful experience this was, to try to show compassion to these people who had been through such harrowing trials. (The chairperson of this volunteer committee was a fellow medical student named Lynn. Thirty years later, I moved to her hometown and we resumed our friendship!)

Several months after Joseph was born, Ed and I began to think about planning our family. Early in our relationship I had assumed that I would be infertile due to cycle irregularities, but I had taken the birth control pill for a short time early on…just to be sure. Disturbing side effects led me to discontinue that. I noticed visual disturbances, e.g., loss of my peripheral vision, and I immediately suspected the pill. After discontinuing it, my vision returned to normal, thanks be to God.

Other women are not so fortunate in the side effects they endure from hormonal contraception. A study published in 2016 found a 70 percent increased risk of depression in women who start oral contraceptives (OC), and researchers in Denmark found that OC users were approximately two to three times more likely to attempt or commit suicide. A 2014 review of the world's literature found the risk of blood clots, leading to potential life-threatening pulmonary emboli for OC users is 3.5 times the risk for non-users. Breast cancer, liver cancer, and cervical cancer risk all increase with use of OCs; in fact, the World Health Organization declared OCs Group 1 carcinogens in 2005. If that isn't enough, how about weight gain and a decrease in libido and attraction to one's spouse? (Maybe that's the way the pill works!) Finally, in approximately 10 percent of cycles of women on the pill, ovulation occurs during the week they take the placebo pills. In this case, the mechanism of action is thinning of the lining of the uterus so a new life cannot implant, thus causing an early abortion. If more young women knew these facts, maybe they would stop using OCs.[9]

---

[9] Kathleen M. Raviele, M.D., "Dangers of Hormonal Birth Control," *Columbia* magazine, July 2018, 25.

Obviously, Ed and I now knew I could get pregnant so what were we to do? One day I noticed an item in the church bulletin announcing a weekend class on natural family planning (NFP). I must have forgotten my disdain for this idea at our Pre-Cana class. The naturalness of this now appealed to me. I had become one of the early Mother Earth types, recycling, reusing…a green, nature child. Wow! A way to space babies naturally, no chemicals, no appliances! I was intrigued and signed us up for the class, taught by the Couple to Couple League (CCL). What a wealth of information we learned from that weekend class series. We learned how the female reproductive system works, how hormones control every detail of a woman's cycle, what bodily signs indicate fertility or infertility and how to read these signs. We were taught how to use this knowledge to either postpone or achieve pregnancy. This is true empowerment for women, to know their own bodies; sadly, the majority of women are not taught this information.

As the class progressed, I was more and more impressed with the science behind the method, but I was more and more annoyed by the teaching couple's continual references to Church teaching and God's plan for marital fertility. I wanted none of it. Once again, the "Great Confusion" in the Catholic Church in those days had affected me personally and blinded me to the beauty of God's design in marriage—which, sadly, was not widely taught. I had no understanding of that beauty, but I became convinced that this natural method could really work at spacing children.

My faithful husband was more than happy to comply. As a cradle Catholic, he desired to follow the Church's teaching that artificial birth control is sinful, but he knew I didn't agree. NFP became the answer for both of us; he could follow his conscience, and I could avoid health risks from artificial contraception. It wasn't always easy and we didn't completely trust the method at first. Abstinence in fertile times can be difficult, and sometimes the signs of fertility were confusing for us.

But something surprising happened along the way. God's grace entered our marriage in a way we had not experienced before. The longer we practiced NFP, the more we trusted in God. The more we trusted in God, the more His truth in the Church's teaching became clear and reasonable. "Those who trust in Him shall understand truth..." (Wisdom 3:9). The beauty of faithfully following God's Church was revealed to us. "Faith precedes understanding"—there it was again. By obedience to Church teaching, even obedience for health reasons, we began to understand the wisdom and beauty of this ancient, yet current teaching. The Church's vision of human sexuality is truly liberating in the freedom from contraception's negative side effects, while reveling in the beauty of our sexuality and the precious gift of cooperating with God in the procreation of human life. We still had a ways to go, but God was once again leading us (me) in His gentle, small steps.

Life was full of learning new things. When Joseph was about six months old, the head nurse at my unit asked me to return to work. I put it off for three more months, then relented when he was nine months old. Now I had to learn how to be a working mother. Living amongst many foreign students and their families, we found a wonderful mother from Syria to care for Joseph while I worked. I cried buckets of tears upon leaving him, and he reacted by promptly weaning himself from nursing.

About this time, Ed became increasingly disillusioned with the medical profession. Having a child brought it home to him that he could not be as involved in our family life as much as he would like. Also, he felt that he did not fit in with the hospital environment. He began to think about other ways he might earn a living, and in the middle of his third year of medical school he took a leave of absence. He suggested we travel to see his close childhood friend, Jim, who lived in Phoenix, in an effort to get away to meditate and discern God's will. This meant I had to leave my nursing job, which I enjoyed very much, but I also enjoyed travel and adventure!

We packed up Joseph and off we went in our little Toyota Tercel.

Ed never returned to medical school. This was agreeable to me as I had remained hesitant about having a physician as a husband. I carried with me the memories from nursing school of the residents' and attending physicians' lives, how busy they were. It may have been selfish of me, but I wanted more time with my husband. Even though we had hoped to work together one day in the medical field, I was fine with abandoning that plan and began to believe that God would show us what the next step in our married life would be.

Ed was hired as a field engineer for the Grand Haven Board of Light and Power to help in building their new municipal power plant. We moved to Grand Haven, a town on Lake Michigan, where I was able to get a nursing job at the small community hospital. I also dabbled in continuing my education, with the goal of earning a bachelor's degree in nursing. (I had graduated from a three-year diploma program.) After several classes, I experienced a crisis of uncertainty. Is this God's will for me? I even took a secretarial course with thoughts of changing careers. Leaving Joseph with the sitter while I worked and went to school tugged at my mother's heart. I was not happy. It was a pivotal point in my life; what direction should I take? I had planned on a nursing career. So why was I not happy in this plan? Ed had never made me feel guilty for working as a nurse; rather, he was proud of me and encouraged me. All I know is that God was shaping me, leading me with His grace into His plan for my life. I began to dread going to work and I didn't register for more nursing classes.

One day as Joseph was playing in our living room and I was watching him, filled with delight at his antics, an unexpected thought came to mind. "We could have another child!" I had been so wrapped up in my turmoil over the direction of my life that this had not occurred to me until that moment. I realized that the greatest joy in my life at that time stemmed from being a mother and caring for Joseph, not from my work as a nurse. God was continuing to "incline my heart according to His will."

Ed was happy at my desire for another child, and we were eager to see if this NFP stuff worked in reverse. Our Mother, the Church, is so wise! I have been blessed to experience the awe of loving marital union realizing that this particular act is likely to result in the creation of an eternal soul, beloved by God. This openness to life imbues the whole experience of marital intimacy with an aura of sacredness that is absent when the possibility of a child's conception is unwanted. This is emphasized so beautifully in Catholic teaching:

In God's divine plan the marital act unites spouses in love and gives rise to new life. God has established an "inseparable connection" between these unitive and procreative purposes of marital love, so when a couple rejects one of these beautiful purposes of their sexual union they harm their spouse and their marriage, even if their intentions are good.[10]

Pope St. John Paul II went even further when he wrote in his *Theology of the Body*, "When the conjugal act is deprived of *its inner truth* because it is deprived artificially of its procreative capacity, it also ceases to be an act of love."[11] How can "making love" cease to be an act of love? Bishop Athanasius Schneider explains:

> The act of transmitting human life is...not an issue exclusively between the two spouses, but refers always to God, the Creator of life. Hence, this act has to be accomplished as God intended it and created it. God...and not man, established the structure and order of human sexuality....The meaning of the sexual act is by its nature procreative; it is meant to give life.

---

[10] "An Introduction to Church Teaching on Contraception," www.hli.org, January 24, 2014, accessed October 21, 2020.

[11] www.hli.org, accessed October 21, 2020

Giving life is something completely selfless, and this should always be the disposition of man and wife in the marital act—selflessness.

Openness to life protects the couple in their sexual union from selfishness. Selfishness is the deadly poison of love. Consequently, when a husband and wife exclude the giving of life in the sexual encounter, they ultimately do not perform an act of love in the way God intends it, but an act of mutual selfishness. And this deeply wounds their love, because every time they exclude new life in the sexual encounter, they become increasingly more selfish.

God wisely made the life-giving act of procreation inseparable from the marital act *in order to protect conjugal love* (emphasis mine)....Openness to life protects spouses from the negative, selfish consequences of original sin.[12]

If either the procreative OR the unitive purpose of marriage is intentionally lacking, the spouses do damage to one another and to their relationship. This is obvious if the *unitive* aspect is missing, as for example, with unrealistic, frequent requests for the marriage act, or in lustful, repugnant

---

[12] Athanasius Schneider and Diane Montagna, *Christus Vincit* (Brooklyn: Angelico Press, Ltd., 2019), 177.

demands of a spouse. It is more subtle but none the less real if the *procreative* aspect is missing. It affects women's identity, and distorts male-female relationships. Sex becomes detached from its natural end, and leads toward an attitude of using the other person for one's own enjoyment.[13]

Let's think about women's identity. What is the most obvious difference between men and women? Women's ability to bear and nourish children. If this ability is first, devalued and denigrated, then artificially reduced, and even in some cases prohibited through contraception, men's and women's separate identities can become blurred and seen as more sameness than differentness. Could this faulty view of sameness between men and women contribute in some way to "the number who identify as LGBT? [This] has been steadily increasing with each generation, according to Gallup. The number grew from 2 percent or less of those born before 1965 to 9.1 percent of Millennials. That has since spiked to 15.9 percent of Generation Z or those born since 1997."[14]

Though facts may not matter greatly to those with ideological agendas, "…there is overwhelming scientific evidence that the brains of men and women exhibit observable

---

[13] www.hli.org, accessed October 21, 2020

[14] Jon Brown, "Number of Young Americans Who Identify as LGBT Skyrockets: Poll," The Daily Wire, www.DailyWire.com (accessed February 25, 2021)

physical differences that result in innate psychological differences. These differences are numerous and complex."[15]

According to Willis Renuart, writing in *Public Discourse*, considering the investment women make in bearing and nurturing children, a civilized society should give them a superior position. Civility in any society depends on the degree to which men and women respect the dignity of women. When the superior position of women is not recognized, both sexes pay a high price.[16] In his General Audience of November 24, 1982 Pope Saint John Paul II said "It is the duty of every man to uphold the dignity of every woman." Renuart continues:

> The freedom and even safety of women depend on men's yielding a certain deference that is based on a clear-eyed appreciation of the differences between the sexes. We want our daughters to have the same opportunities as our sons, but that is not possible unless women are first treated with the respect that only comes from recognizing the differences between

---

[15] Willis Renuart, "To Control 'Toxic Masculinity' and Heal the Family We Must Appreciate the Differences between the Sexes," *Public Discourse*, The Witherspoon Institute, www.thepublicdiscourse.com (accessed February 25, 2021).

[16] Renuart, www.thepublicdiscourse.com (accessed February 27, 2021).

the sexes. Our present lack of civility can be explained by a general failure of our society to recognize women's dignity. This is caused by many factors, including...*advances in modern birth control* (my emphasis) that have freed women to behave more like men. All these things have also made it harder to form monogamous long-term relationships, because the traditions and restraints that had previously enhanced the position of women have been undermined.[17]

Ed and I had not thought through all these ideas, but we did try to be faithful to Church teaching in our marriage. When our second child was conceived, we trusted all the more in NFP, seeing it work both to postpone and to achieve pregnancy. We talked about sharing this good news with others and decided to apply to become a teaching couple with the Couple to Couple League. After months of study, we were certified as teachers and began what turned out to be over 20 years of teaching natural family planning and speaking at Pre-Cana weekends to engaged couples. It was at one such Pre-Cana that I came full circle from our own Pre-Cana years earlier. Remember how I had proudly asserted to Ed that NFP

---

[17] Ibid.

was just the same as contraception, as the end goal is the same? One couple asked this specific question and we were able to explain the difference with an analogy. If I needed a certain amount of money, I could either work to earn the money, or I could rob a bank to get the money. One means is honorable and produces virtue; the other is gravely sinful. Using contraception is sinful—as explained earlier—while practicing NFP explicitly calls for self-giving and sacrifice for the good of the other. The "end" may be the same—avoiding pregnancy—but the means are very different. The Church also reminds couples that attempts to regulate births, even with NFP, must be done with a loving, generous spirit, open to life, while responding to God's call for their particular family.

Teaching NFP initiated us into the cadre of those willing to be counter-cultural. We were proponents of a method that was not only scoffed at by secular culture, the medical field, and our family, but was ridiculed and denied even by most Catholics. According to the Pew Research Center in 2016, nearly 90 percent of American Catholics believe contraception is morally acceptable or not a moral issue at all.[18] In 1973, about five years before Ed and I married, 66.3 percent of white Catholic married couples reported utilizing artificial

---

[18] Jessica Weinberger, "NFP and Creation Care," *Family Foundations*, July/August 2020, 18.

contraception.[19] In an April 2011 study by the Guttmacher Institute, among women aged 15-44 who had sex in the last three months but weren't pregnant, postpartum, or trying to get pregnant, 87 percent of women who identified as Catholic used contraception.[20] This same study indicated that "only two percent currently used natural family planning."[21]

The Catholic perspective has not been taken seriously by Catholics themselves. In most dioceses, the Church's teachings on contraception receive almost no treatment from the pulpit and are given an hour or two during a marriage-preparation class. Given the centrality of the issue, and the centrality of sexuality to the human person, this is not an acceptable situation.[22] When I asked a local priest to host an NFP class in his parish, he told me *he didn't believe in it.*

---

[19] Kathleen Ford, "Contraceptive Utilization-United States," *Vital and Health Statistics-Series 23-No. 2, DHEW Publication No. (PHS) 79-1978* (September 1979), www.cdc.gov (accessed November 4, 2020).

[20] Molly Hemingway, "Lies, Damned Lies and 98 Percent of Catholic Women," *Get Religion* (February 14, 2012), www.getreligion.org (accessed November 4, 2020).

[21] Glenn Kessler, "The Claim that 98 Percent of Catholic Women Use Contraception: A Media Foul," *The Washington Post* (February 17, 2012) www.washingtonpost.com (accessed November 4, 2020).

[22] Timothy Reichert, "Bitter Pill," *First Things*, www.firstthings.com/article/2010/05/bitter-pill (accessed January 2, 2021).

But we did believe in it! Our experience of the effectiveness of NFP also birthed a slow-growing skepticism of the mainstream medical field. Up until this time, I was a firm believer in all I had learned in nursing school. But there had been no mention of modern fertility awareness, only the promotion of artificial contraception and denigration of "calendar rhythm" (an earlier form of fertility awareness based on historical cycle length, which has a lower effectiveness rate than modern natural family planning methods). The medical establishment seemed completely ignorant of this marvelous scientific knowledge of fertility awareness, which when applied through the method that CCL taught, is over 99 percent effective in postponing pregnancy.[23] If they are ignorant of this, what else are they ignorant of?

By the time the nausea intensified with my second pregnancy I had decided to quit my nursing job and abandon thoughts of pursuing a higher degree. My thoughts shifted to learning more about mothering, specifically how to avoid another C-section. My obstetrician assured me I could try a VBAC (vaginal birth after cesarean), but without the proper education and guidance, our daughter, Heidi Fae Stuart, was eventually born via C-section on October 7, 1982. Ed was still agreeable about me choosing our daughter's first name.

---

[23] What is Natural Family Planning?" Couple to Couple League, www.ccli.org (accessed November 4, 2020.

"Katie" had vanished by this time, but my warm memories of reading the children's version of *Heidi* by Johanna Spyri as a young child inspired me to name her "Heidi." We agreed that "Fae" would go nicely as a middle name.

I developed endometritis (an inflammatory condition of the lining of the uterus, usually due to an infection) soon after her birth and the doctor told me it was because I labored before having the C-section. That made me feel guilty. I was not allowed to hold Heidi or nurse her for the first several days, and tears flowed down my face as I watched Ed feed her a glucose solution out in the hallway. It all seemed rather barbaric to me and I couldn't wait to be out of the hospital and home with our beautiful daughter. I was totally in love with her! She took to nursing as well as her older brother did, and he showered much affection on his new sister. We were a happy family!

5
Infant to Toddler to School Age ... Then What?

Joseph was now nearing the age when many parents consider a pre-school for their child. I followed this trend, and enrolled him for a short time in a local Montessori program. I hadn't given much thought to his education overall; I fully expected that he would attend the local public school when it was time. But Ed had different ideas. While living in Alaska, he had been introduced to the idea of homeschooling. "...Hundreds or perhaps thousands of homesteading families live many miles from the nearest town, or even road. The only way they can get in and out of their homes is by plane. Since the state cannot provide schools for these families..."[24] they teach their children themselves. This was a novel idea to me and one which I initially rejected. I was selfishly imagining all the free time I would have at home with Joseph at school!

Once again, God showed up...this time at the public library. Joseph and I were strolling through the aisles of books when a book literally fell off the shelf in front of me. I picked it up and read the title, *Teach Your Own*, by John Holt. I wasn't familiar with the author but the title was intriguing.

---

[24] John Holt, *Teach Your Own* (Dell Publishing Co, Inc., 1981), 53.

5 *Infant to Toddler to School Age...Then What?*

Does this mean teaching one's own children, as in a school? Is this what Ed was talking about? I would soon find out as I brought the book home and immersed myself in it. This book was about to make an impact on my life and my family's life as great as any decision we had made. *Teach Your Own* convinced me with the utmost certainty that homeschooling was the path God was calling us to.

Specifically, it was the first chapter that convinced me. It is entitled, "Why Take Them Out?" All of these reasons resonated deeply with me. The very first paragraph reads:

> Why do people take or keep their children out of school? Mostly for three reasons: they think that raising their children is their business not the governments's; they enjoy being with their children and watching and helping them learn, and don't want to give that up to others; and they want to keep them from being hurt, mentally, physically, and spiritually.

The first reason: without knowing until years later that the Church teaches that parents are the primary educators of their children, I felt it intuitively. This meshes nicely with Pope St. John Paul II's call to responsible parenthood—seeking God's will in regard to family size and using natural fertility awareness methods if there is a serious need to space or avoid children. Responsible parenthood doesn't just mean discerning if and when to procreate though; it means educating one's children, especially in the life of faith. *Teach Your Own*'s secular author, John Holt, expresses it this way:

> Even though many and perhaps most adults today dislike and distrust children, there is at the same time a growing minority of people who like, understand, trust, respect, and value children in a way rarely known until now.
>
> Many of these people are *choosing* to have children as few people before ever did. They don't have children just because that is what married people are supposed to do, or because they don't know how not to have them. On the contrary, knowing well what it may mean in time, energy, money, thought, and worry, they undertake the heavy responsibility of having and bringing up children because they deeply want to spend a part of their life living with them. Having chosen to have children, they feel very strongly that it is *their* responsibility to help these children grow into good, smart, capable, loving, trustworthy, and responsible human beings. They do not think it right to turn that responsibility over to institutions, state or private, schools or otherwise, and

would not do so, even if they liked and trusted these institutions, which on the whole they do not.[25]

The second reason: I had been so enjoying raising my first child I desired another. And I so enjoyed teaching my first child and instilling our values in this child, that I was not going to abdicate that responsibility. As Joseph came of school age and I considered his attendance at the local school, I pondered these questions: How do I know what the teacher is teaching him? What is he or she saying to him? How will my son be formed by this teacher? I realized I didn't know the answers to these questions and the only way I would know for certain what Joseph would be taught is if we taught him ourselves.

The third reason: being reminded of the ways that my own public school experiences were hurtful was a great incentive to protect my children from similar mental, physical, and spiritual harm. Though I had escaped from gross incompetence of schools—one form of mental harm—the numbers of children who do not are legion.

Results of the 2019 National Assessment of Educational Progress (NAEP), which tested grades 4, 8, and 12, showed that just about *one in three* U.S. 12th graders read proficiently

---

[25] Holt, 21-22.

and *less than one in four* are proficient in math. [Emphasis mine.] U.S. Secretary of Education Betsy DeVos said in a statement:

> Sadly, [these] results confirm America's schools continue to fall far short, and continue to fail too many kids, especially the most disadvantaged. Being a high school graduate should mean something. But when 40% of these graduates are 'below basic' in math, and 30% are 'below basic' in reading, it's hard to argue the education system is preparing them for what comes next.[26]

Additionally, U.S. students historically do poorly on international assessments compared to many foreign peers. And it's estimated that more than one-third of all college students, and more than one-half in community colleges, need some remedial help, according to research from the Teachers College at Columbia University.[27]

---

[26] Dr. Susan Berry, "Teachers' Union Seeks More Funding as Pre-Pandemic Nation's Report Card Reveals More Student Failure," Breitbart News Network, www.breitbart.com (accessed November 2, 2020).

[27] "Nation's Report Card Reveals High School Seniors Lack Critical Math and Reading Skills," The Associated Press, May 7, 2014, www.nydailynews.com (accessed October 26, 2020).

5 Infant to Toddler to School Age...Then What?

Another form of mental harm is emotional harassment and humiliation. A teacher writes:

> I'm especially interested in the "social life" aspect of schools and the damage it causes. This morning I asked my third graders, "Do you feel that in our school kids are nice, kind to each other? Out of 22 kids, only two felt that they saw kindness, and the rest felt that most kids are mean, call names, hurt feelings, etc. Frankly, I was amazed.[28]

The social life of most schools and classrooms is mean-spirited, status-oriented, competitive, and snobbish. According to author, educator, speaker and child advocate John Holt, not *one* person of the hundreds with whom he has discussed this has yet said to him that the social life at school is kindly, generous, supporting, democratic, friendly, loving, or good for children.[29]

Physical harm in schools has progressed from terrorizing and bullying—hitting, pushing, tripping, slapping, spitting, stealing, destroying possessions—to sexual harassment,

---

[28] Holt, 49.

[29] Ibid.

sexual assault,[30] and even death in the increasingly violent culture of school shootings.

The most damaging harm to children occurs in the spiritual realm. "And do not be afraid of those who kill the body but cannot kill the soul; rather, be afraid of the one who can destroy both soul and body in Gehenna" (Matthew 10:28). Undermining the faith life of public school children has been going on for decades. The language of textbooks is one way this is accomplished. Three primary indoctrination methods textbook publishers use to undermine Christianity are the censorship of America's true Christian heritage; association propaganda–the linking of negative ideas or events with Christian principles, people, or groups; and finally, contextual redefinition, which changes the meaning of written text in order to support a preplanned conclusion that is different from the original author's intention.[31]

Possibly the most egregious abuse of parents' trust is the atheistic socialist/communist (I will use these terms interchangeably, as they are both based on Marxist theory) infiltration of the public education system. The complete

---

[30] "Physical Bully," www.bullyingstatistics.org (accessed October 26, 2020).

[31] Michael J. Chapman, "Anti-Christian Bias in Education," June 10, 2008, www.EdWatch.org (accessed October 28, 2020).

breakdown of American education is one of the most distressing things to have happened to our country. These philosophies have successfully infiltrated and corrupted Western society. This is obvious in at least five areas:

Promoting Communist Ideology Among the Young

This ideology gradually took over Western academia by infiltrating important traditional fields of study, as well as fabricating new sciences beholden to its ideological influence. Literature, history, philosophy, social science, anthropology, the study of law, media, and other concentrations have become inundated with various derivatives of Marxist theory. "Political correctness" became the guideline for censoring free thought on campuses.

Reducing the Young Generation's Exposure to Traditional Culture

Orthodox thought, genuine history, and classical literature have been slandered and marginalized in many different ways. Common justifications for this include arguments that the classics are no longer relevant to modern students, or that school curricula need to make room for more "diversity" of thought.

Lowering Academic Standards Starting in Primary School

Because instruction has been progressively dumbed down, students of the new generation are becoming less literate and mathematically capable. They possess less knowledge, and their ability to think critically is stunted. It is hard for these students to handle key questions concerning life and society in a logical and forthright manner, and even harder for them to see through socialism's deceptions.

Indoctrinating Young Students With Deviated Notions

As these children grow older, the degrading concepts instilled in them become so strong that it is nearly impossible to identify and correct them.

Feeding Students' Selfishness, Greed, and Indulgence

This includes conditioning them to oppose authority and tradition, inflating their egos and sense of entitlement, reducing their ability to understand and tolerate different opinions, and neglecting their psychological growth.[32]

Communism also works to achieve its goal of destroying human morality. The distortion and downward spiral of the moral standards of American youth are no accident. Communism forcibly spreads atheism in schools as a means of destroying morality. In America, the public education system ejected belief in God from schools under the pretext of upholding the separation of church and state. Through various means, this pulls children away from parents with religious beliefs. This is the most challenging problem that families

---

[32] "How the Specter of Communism is Ruling Our World," Part 1, Chapter 12, *The Epoch Times*, www.theepochtimes.com (accessed October 28, 2020). Used with permission.

with religious beliefs face when it comes to their children's education, and it's the most evil aspect of the anti-theistic education system.[33] What a contrast from the days when the "Bible Lady" came to my country school to teach the Bible!

The following letter was written by Mary Kay Clark, director of Seton Home Study School, to the parents of their enrolled students. Though it would be years in the making as Ed and I both grew in our faith, this is what we hoped for in our family. Dr. Clark writes:

> *Inside your Catholic home, you provide an environment in which knowing, loving, and serving God is respected and protected. Inside your home, you teach about the wonder of life and the wonder of the universe. You instill in them the love of God, the love of life, and the love of learning that they will cherish all their lives.*
>
> *Pope St. John Paul II always maintained that a new springtime is coming in the Church. When this springtime arrives, and you look around and see people renewed with spiritual vigor, please do me a favor. Think back on the days and nights spent teaching your children. Recall the hours spent*

---

[33] Ibid.

sounding out letters in phonics. Remember the joy of re-reading a favorite book from your youth as you help your child with a book report. When this springtime arrives, breathe in the scent of this new spiritual bouquet. Think back to your days of homeschooling, and say to yourself, "I helped." You are quietly changing the world. You are changing America. Most importantly, you are changing your children.

Pope St. Paul VI once said, "Every mother is like Moses. She does not enter the Promised Land. She prepares a world she will not see."

6
Alaska, North Dakota, and Three New Christians

So I began my sojourn like Moses. I remember commenting to Ed at the beginning of our homeschooling adventure: "If we do this, it will be one of the most challenging and important things we do in our lives."

Even the most challenging endeavor begins with the first step. Beginning homeschooling with very young children is quite simple. Don't send them to school, and keep doing what you have been doing: talking with them, modeling manners and kindness, playing together, exploring nature together, and a myriad of other common parent-child activities. Ed and I basically just continued living our life, including our children in that life. We didn't know much about homeschooling yet, but as was the pattern for much of my life, when I needed to know something, I turned to books to learn. Holt's *Teach Your Own* was the most important initially, with books by Dr. Raymond and Dorothy Moore (*Better Late Than Early*, *Home Style Teaching*, *Home Grown Kids*, *The Successful Homeschool Family Handbook*) forming our early approaches. But now, at this point in our family, we just lived life!

6 Alaska, North Dakota, and Three New Christians

With our two children in tow, we moved to an old farmhouse out in the country east of Grand Haven. It was my first return to rural living after leaving home and I loved it there. Here was the first of many gardens...a big garden that I planned myself. (My mother and Grandma Alice drove clear across the state to help me plant it. I suppose they did want to see our new daughter too!) We had recently acquired a Manx cat so this house would be dubbed the "Kitty House." She was a gentle cat and seemed to enjoy it when Joseph would lay his head on her tummy or when Heidi would pull her (short) tail when crawling around on the floor. The cat was a terror to the neighbor's dog though; one day I heard the dog howling in our yard with the cat on his back clawing and biting him. He never came back! I began to learn how to can food at this house and settled into my new identity as a housewife and mother. My father often reminded me that he found it comical when I called my mother to ask how to get the peel off peaches before canning them. (They have to be perfectly ripe...otherwise it's a mess!)

Ed's employment looked as if it would come to an end when the power plant construction was finished so he began thinking about what to do next. Alaska was always in the back of his mind, but he liked the Midwest too, especially the northern tier. He put out some feelers first by calling the engineering department at the University of North Dakota in

6 Alaska, North Dakota, and Three New Christians

Grand Forks. He inquired if they were aware of any engineering firms in the area hiring. After chatting for some time with Mr. Dixon, the chairman of the electrical engineering department, Ed was surprised when the chairman told him that they had a faculty position open at the university. Ed had a Master's degree, but not a Ph.D., which is normally required at universities, so he had never considered the possibility of teaching at an engineering school. What an intriguing opportunity!

The chairman, Mr. Dixon, invited Ed and me and the kids to Grand Forks for an interview in the summer of 1983. Not in the habit of doing things in the usual way, we decided to take the Amtrak (yes, with a three-year-old and nine-month-old). It was a hot summer as I recall, and the air conditioning on the train felt very good...until nighttime. I hadn't brought a sweater or jacket as it had been so hot; I didn't even have anything warm for the kids, so Ed went off wandering through the train in the dark looking for something to keep us warm. He returned some time later and put something over me as I held Heidi in my arms. "Oh, thank you, Dear, that feels nice and warm." In the morning when light returned I was able to see the well-worn floor mat that Ed had put over us in the night! He was definitely an unconventional kind of guy! And I loved that fact.

6 Alaska, North Dakota, and Three New Christians

I remember looking out the Amtrak windows as we neared Grand Forks. I hadn't traveled to this part of the country before and I was amazed at the flat land all around, as far as the eye could see. Little clumps of trees around farmhouses and the rest all grains, sugar beets, and beans. The university put us up in a hotel and we toured the beautiful campus. Ed must have done a good job at the interview because they offered him the job. He did not accept the offer; he said he had to think about it. I tried not to interfere, as I knew he was still holding out for the possibility of moving to Alaska.

When we returned home he called a friend in Alaska and the friend said there was a job at the Army base where Ed had been stationed previously. That was all it took. Ed called Mr. Dixon and declined the job offer, gave his notice at the power plant, and began planning our move to Alaska. He knew many things about what we would need and how to prepare to live there that I did not know, so he concentrated on preparations while I packed and planned the details of family life along the way. I wanted to spend some time back at home on the farm with my parents before leaving for who might know how long, and Ed planned to modify his pickup truck so we could bring necessary belongings with us. He could work on that on the farm with my brother Randy's help.

6 Alaska, North Dakota, and Three New Christians

Ed also wanted to take one last trip before committing to Alaska—out east to Maine. So off we went, the four of us in the little Toyota again, traveling through Canada to northern Maine, New Hampshire, Vermont, and New York. We stopped at Niagara Falls and then returned to Michigan. It was a fun trip and we have lovely pictures of it.

When we arrived home, there was big news. My father, 56 years old and a farmer all his life, felt God calling him to the ministry. He had spoken to a local pastor and gotten the name of a seminary in Jackson, Mississippi. This school would intensify my father's tendencies toward anti-Catholicism and would lead to heartache in the future, but we were ignorant of that at the time. We were happy for them. Now there were two families preparing for major life changes. My parents put their house up for sale and it sold quickly. Randy took over the farm—my younger brother, Ken, had moved to Minneapolis earlier—and in late October 1983, my parents left for Mississippi while Ed and I and the kids left for Alaska in our pickup truck. We looked like the Beverly Hillbillies, with high side boards on the truck and all kinds of supplies stacked to the top, covered with a tarp.

Our initial destination was Ken's apartment in Minneapolis, where he lived with his family. We planned to spend a few days with them and make sure the truck and its load were secure. Our first morning there, we realized that we had forgotten about the home-canned food and large quantity of potatoes we had piled in the pickup. They were frozen solid! Well, we decided to haul them along anyway and feed them to Ed's friends' pigs in Alaska.

About this time, Heidi was a year old and my fertility had returned. CCL taught a method of caring for one's baby, called ecological breastfeeding, that I practiced. The basic tenets of this method include:

—Breastfeed exclusively for baby's first six months.

—Pacify and comfort baby at the breast.

—Don't use bottles or pacifiers.

—Sleep with baby for night feedings.

—Sleep with baby for daily nap feeding.

—Nurse frequently, day and night, and avoid schedules.

—Avoid any practice that restricts nursing or separates mother from baby.

By following these practices, the average return of menstruation for mothers after childbirth in the North American culture is between 14 and 15 months.[34]

Ed and I were considering, but not very seriously, another child. Many faithful couples who practice NFP come to open their hearts to the gift of life such that following the rules

---

[34] Sheila Kippley, "The Seven Standards Summary," Natural Family Planning International, Inc., www.nfpandmore.org (accessed November 8, 2020).

6 Alaska, North Dakota, and Three New Christians

doesn't always take precedence over the loving look of a husband and wife. We knew I was fertile during this time of travel to Alaska...and God blessed us with pregnancy number three! This put a new twist on things; if I was true to form, I would be sick within three weeks. But hope springs eternal; maybe this time it would be different! For now, I felt great and I was eagerly anticipating this great adventure.

We decided that the kids and I should fly from Minneapolis to Edmonton, Alberta and meet Ed there. It's a long way across Canada to Delta Junction, Alaska! He wanted to shorten the time spent in the truck with all four of us. So several days after Ed headed out in the pickup, Ken dropped us off at the airport and we flew to Edmonton. Ed met us and we left there with him driving, a baby seat with Heidi buckled in the middle, and Joseph and I buckled in the one other seat belt. Heidi had developed a diaper rash and I have memories of changing her sore little bottom on the pickup seat in the freezing temperatures of Canada in November.

We were headed for the great Alcan! Today the road from Dawson Creek, British Columbia to Delta Junction, Alaska is known as the Alaska Highway, but in those days it was known as the Alcan. Looking at a current map of Canada, one sees that beginning at Dawson Creek, British Columbia, heading northwest to the Yukon and into Alaska, there is one and only one road. This is an area of vast wilderness and beauty, with forests and swamps and permafrost. The Alaska Highway, built in 1942, was the engineering marvel of World War II and was once described as the largest and most difficult construction project since the Panama Canal.[35] For eight months, the lives of 18,000 men and women were dominated by The Road, and for most, it would remain one of the highlights of their lives.[36]

Today the road is all paved or chip sealed, but when we traveled, it was gravel and a rough, challenging drive. This road is 1,382 miles long! There are few places to purchase supplies or fuel, so one is required to plan carefully before embarking on this journey. We took a picture of the sign in Dawson Creek which said "YOU ARE NOW ENTERING THE WORLD FAMOUS ALASKA HIGHWAY." It pointed us in the right direction (which veteran Alcan traveler Ed already knew), venturing NNW into the great wilderness. We passed through Fort St. John, then Fort Nelson and on to Summit Lake. This is a breathtakingly beautiful spot. I remember the crisp, clear morning with the ground covered in snow, the lake sparkling at the base of the surrounding hills.

---

[35] "Alaska Highway," Bell's Travel Guides, www.bellsalaska.com (accessed November 8, 2020).

[36] Murray Lundberg, "Alaska Highway or Alcan? And where is Mile 0?" www.explorenorth.com/library/roads/ alcan-signs.html (accessed November 1, 2020).

6 Alaska, North Dakota, and Three New Christians

The history is rich here; Ed explained that the lake was a jumping-off point for the fur traders heading north into the Northwest Territories a century earlier.

I have no memory of the details of eating or sleeping on our journey; we were both frugal people, so it's likely we slept in the truck and fed peanut butter and jelly sandwiches to the kids! When we reached Whitehorse, Yukon, a large town, we purchased foodstuffs and hiked around. I have a picture of us in the Catholic cemetery.

Somewhere along here, the pickup started malfunctioning. The heater intermittently quit working—with temperatures in the teens—and its speed topped out at about 45 miles per hour. Ed knew basic mechanics but he was not especially proficient in diagnostics. And there weren't any Napa Auto Parts stores on the Alcan! We just prayed and limped along, with the thought that he would see to it when we arrived in Delta Junction.

Thanks be to God, we did arrive safe and sound at our friend's log home out in the woods. They had five children, with the youngest being around Joseph's age. (Some of the older children had left home.) They were such hospitable people that there was another young family of three staying with them too. That meant there were more than ten of us in their home with one indoor bathroom…but there was a well-used outhouse! (One of the most appreciated useful facts

6 Alaska, North Dakota, and Three New Christians

I learned while living there with them was that if you put styrofoam around the toilet seat in the outhouse, the shock of zero degrees is greatly lessened.)

Our first priority was to find work for Ed and then a place to live. He tried to connect with the friend who said there was a job at the base. When that finally happened, he learned the job was actually non-existent. Oh my! So he began a long and nearly fruitless search, though he was offered an engineering job in Fairbanks, which was about 90 miles away. This was not ideal.

While we considered that, we experienced life with our friends—a fundamentalist Christian family. They were part of a Christian community, many of whom actually lived in common at a rural compound. This was my first experience of community life and it made a positive impression on me, even though their theology was much different from Catholicism. Ed and I felt intrigued by this community life, and the interest stayed with us for many years as later we explored the possibility of rural community life for our own family...with the stipulation that it be Catholic.

The guidance of the Catholic Church is so valuable! There are all kinds of theological pitfalls outside the solid doctrine of Catholicism. The young mother of one child who was also staying temporarily with our friends was friendly and welcoming, but when she learned about my C-section

6 Alaska, North Dakota, and Three New Christians

deliveries and that I was Catholic, she proudly said, "If you had more faith, you wouldn't need C-sections." To avoid any tension while living there together, I said nothing—though I certainly told Ed—and we began looking in earnest for other living arrangements.

We checked out a cute little cabin that was under construction along the Tanana River. We would have to live quite rustically for a bit until we could finish it off, but that idea was appealing to me. As we pondered and prayed about this, I realized that the fast-flowing river just down the bank would be a danger to our children. Cross that one off the list. Then another friend of Ed's contacted him and offered us a house-sitting arrangement at his lovely home in Delta Junction while he and his family were in the Lower 48 indefinitely. This was a wonderful offer and we thankfully accepted it and made plans to move there.

Pregnancy nausea had not hit yet, so while Ed was looking for work and finances were becoming tight, I decided to apply at the local health clinic, the only medical care for many miles around. There was one physician (or physician assistant—I can't remember) and one nurse at the clinic. The nurse functioned as receptionist, secretary, lab technician, x-ray technician, and nurse. She was retiring and I thought it would be great experience to learn these various responsibilities. Some time later— I don't remember exactly

6 Alaska, North Dakota, and Three New Christians

when—I was hired! I nervously looked forward to my start day...but wouldn't you know, shortly before that day, the familiar feelings of nausea and fatigue began. I was determined to follow through with this employment however, and went off to work...for one day. I thoroughly enjoyed my co-worker and all that I was learning, but I just could not function as was necessary for the good of the patients. I reluctantly resigned, knowing from experience that my condition would only worsen until at least the mid-point of my pregnancy.

We moved into the house-sitting arrangement and enjoyed having more elbow room. I became more and more debilitated from early pregnancy, and as winter intensified, the increased darkness added to my misery. Daylight began around 10 AM and dusk was upon us by 3 PM. This darkness, more than anything, began to weaken my resolve and my desire for adventure. The lack of light affected me so severely that I talked to Ed about going home. He was disillusioned with the job situation too, and I think he realized it was not likely to improve any time soon, so we agreed to head for home. I was sad to admit this apparent defeat; maybe we didn't allow God enough say in the decision to go to Alaska, or maybe He thought we needed just a taste of adventure, or maybe there was someone in Alaska that we needed to meet. Maybe I wasn't as tough as I thought I was!

6 Alaska, North Dakota, and Three New Christians

Ed thought it best if I flew with the kids back to my brother's in Minneapolis while he drove the pickup home. I remember feeling so sick on the plane, but my travel was nothing compared to my long-suffering husband's travels. Remember the pickup's malfunctioning heater, and the 45-mph top speed? We had completely forgotten to have it repaired. Why did he not stop for repairs when he realized this? I don't know, but by this time, the heater in the truck had stopped working entirely. The following description of his trip is based only on my memory of the experiences he shared with me, experiences that were probably only the tip of the iceberg of all he endured. (Tip of the iceberg—HA!) He said that when he just couldn't take the cold anymore, he would pull off to the side of the road, lift the hood of the truck, and lie across the engine to soak up its heat. As the days passed and the temperatures were plummeting, he chose to go south as quickly as he could, so he headed to Calgary from Edmonton, Alberta. This took him down to Montana, through Great Falls and into Lewistown. By this time I was at Ken's and Ed called me on a pay phone. Sometime in our previous trips, we had discovered Lewistown, Montana and we both loved that little town, nestled in the Judith Mountains. Ed thought taking this southern route, rather than through Canada, would be a bit milder. Not that day. The night he stopped there, the temperature was -30 F. When he stood at

6 Alaska, North Dakota, and Three New Christians

the registration desk at the hotel, the clerk said, "Wow, I knew it was cold out, but I didn't know it was *that* cold!" Ed must have looked quite frozen. He said that he went to the room and turned on the hot water and stood in the shower for a long time!

After such a short stay in Alaska, we must have eaten some humble pie served up by my family, but I don't remember that it was too painful! We stayed with Grandma Alice for several weeks until we could figure out what to do. Ed wondered if he could get work at the power plant in Grand Haven again; nope, that was not available. In desperation and with humility, he called Mr. Dixon from the University of North Dakota (UND) to inquire if the faculty position was still available. The answer came: yes! Ed accepted the position and we were filled with gratitude to God, providing for us even though it seemed we had been a bit foolhardy. God knows us through and through and loves us still!

Until the academic year of 1984 began in the fall and we moved to North Dakota, we rented a small apartment in Grand Rapids to spend some time near Ed's widowed mother. He was able to get regular work with ManPower, which was a welcome income. The apartment was smack dab in the middle of a large commercial district in the city—quite a contrast from the previous months in the Alaskan wilderness. But I always gave thanks to God for providing for us; even here,

6   *Alaska, North Dakota, and Three New Christians*

there was a small patch of wooded land behind all the businesses that the kids and I were able to "hike" on. This apartment had an army of ants which appeared quite regularly in the bathroom, so this domicile was dubbed the "Ant House." We lived quite simply here, with most of our belongings in storage (somewhere; I can't remember where everything was, but I do remember with sorrow that my wedding dress and Ed's suit were lost at this time, never to be found). We slept on twin air mattresses and the kids on the floor. A funny memory of living at the Ant House involved a phone call from a saleslady who tried to convince me to upgrade our phone to a touch-dial phone (we had the old-style dial phone at the time). This seemed like a complete waste of money to me and I asked her why I would want to do that. She said it would be so much faster. I replied, "If I don't have enough time to dial the phone, I am way too busy." We continued to use that old phone until 2011!

 I believe one of the reasons God chose this apartment complex for us was to meet some Vietnamese neighbors upstairs. They were a young family with one small child and they didn't speak English very well yet. The wife worked outside the home while the husband cared for their child. We got to know each other a bit; they were Catholic too. One day near the end of our stay at the Ant House, the husband rushed into our apartment shouting that he had a fire in his kitchen

6 Alaska, North Dakota, and Three New Christians

and had burned his arm! Ed was at work so I quickly ran up to their apartment and surveyed the scene. The kitchen was filled with smoke and the stovetop was a mess of black ash, scorched cooking utensils, and grease. The fire appeared to be out, so I focused on his burned arm. It looked nasty and would need medical attention. He had called his wife and she was on her way home, but I knew they didn't have knowledge of the area hospitals. As soon as she arrived, I suggested that if she would bring her child down to our apartment and watch our children, I would drive her husband to the Emergency Department. This was agreed upon, so I took him to my alma mater, Butterworth Hospital, and stayed with him until he was discharged. By this time, I was in my third trimester of pregnancy and getting more and more uncomfortable, but moving day was upon us. This lovely young Vietnamese wife came to our apartment on her own initiative that day and completely packed up our whole kitchen. What a blessing that was to me!

Off we went to Grand Forks, North Dakota. Ed drove a moving truck—no Amtrak this time—while I drove our new red Jeep Cherokee. (We traded in the little Toyota, as it was not big enough for three children in the back seat. Four years later when baby number four came along, we installed a seat belt in the very back of the Jeep and buckled a baby seat in there—backwards!) We moved into a faculty housing

6 Alaska, North Dakota, and Three New Christians

apartment complex with a swimming pool! We now had three bedrooms and felt like royalty. UND treated Ed very well and he took to teaching like a duck to water; after all his years of searching for his niche, he'd finally found it! He enjoyed teaching and was very much appreciated by his students, even being nominated for Professor of the Year. The kids loved the swimming pool and I enjoyed watching their different approaches to water. While Joseph was more cautious about swimming, not so Heidi! At 21 months old she ran and leapt right into the pool, wearing her water wings. The pool was a favorite activity for Ed and the kids.

I needed to find an obstetrician quite soon, as baby's due date was nearing. I must have just picked one out of the phone book. After several visits, the doctor said I needed to have an amniocentesis—a procedure in which a small sample of amniotic fluid is drawn out of the uterus through a needle inserted into the abdomen. The fluid is then analyzed to detect genetic abnormalities in the fetus. There was no way I was going to agree to this. I knew that there were potential hazards, including infection, bleeding, leakage of amniotic fluid, miscarriage, and injury to the baby. And I didn't need to know if there was any abnormality in our child. I was quite upset and emotional about this and called Ed at work and cried. I should have taken to heart Pope St. John Paul II's repeated assurance: "Be not afraid!" Within a couple of days,

6 Alaska, North Dakota, and Three New Christians

my labor kicked in and all thoughts of needing an amniocentesis vanished, praise be to God!

I labored through the night even though I was planning a C-section—the OB doctor on call was busy with another delivery. When he was finally available, he gave orders for me to have a general anesthesia for the surgery (I had epidural anesthesia for the two previous births). When I asked why, I was told that "there wasn't enough time for an epidural." Hmmm, I thought, not enough time for what? I've been laboring away here for quite some time. I never got an answer to that question, but it was all forgotten upon waking up to see our beautiful new daughter, born on July 23, 1984, and named Rachel Claire Stuart. Her name was first considered when we lived at the Ant House. I read a book entitled *Rachel Weeping—The Case Against Abortion*, by James T. Burtchaell. It not only reinforced my convictions about the immorality of abortion, but I was very moved by the Bible verse, Matthew 2:18, which referred to the Holy Innocents slaughtered in place of Jesus by Herod and which inspired the book's title: "A voice was heard in Ramah, sobbing and loud lamentation; Rachel weeping for her children, and she would not be consoled, since they were no more." "Claire" came from watching *Brother Sun, Sister Moon*, a 1972 film about St. Francis and St. Clare that Ed and I had seen while courting.

6 *Alaska, North Dakota, and Three New Christians*

Ed was very sleepy that morning so he dozed off and on while I nursed Rachel. She was so cute, with the standard Stuart round face which the previous two had had. At one point, Ed jumped up and asked me when Grandma Alice was supposed to arrive. We both had completely forgotten that she was arriving on the Amtrak that morning to stay with us for a week and help care for our family. He rushed off to the train station and found my dear grandmother, who had been patiently waiting for five hours at the station! (This was long before cell phones.) She took it all with humor and was delighted at the reason for our forgetfulness—our little Rachel!

Early that winter, we decided to look for a house to purchase—our first. We found a yellow (my favorite color) 1½ story house on a dead-end street adjacent to a park. Just perfect! The backyard abutted the Red River of the North, which is notorious for springtime flooding, so there was a dike along the back property line. (Long after we had moved away from this house, I saw it on the evening news with water up to the second floor windows as the Red River flooded that year. Our entire neighborhood was demolished and is now vacant land next to the park.) We could look across the river into Minnesota, and the kids enjoyed sledding down the dike. There was room for a clothesline and a large garden—necessary features for me. The dirt here was so black and rich that next summer when we grew squash, the plants were taller than me!

We settled into our new home, joining the UND campus parish with a Newman Center and a dynamic priest. I was adjusting to caring for three children five and under and incorporating teaching moments into our daily routine. Joseph was not interested in learning to read yet but he enjoyed our numerous story-times throughout the day and Ed was always talking to him and explaining how things work.

Our new pastor's preaching and teaching were challenging both of us, but especially me, to grow in our faith. He wanted us to take a Baptism class for parents. Finally, God's grace broke through my stubbornness and I was able to accept Catholic teaching on infant Baptism. The *Catechism of the Catholic Church* (CCC) says the two principal effects of Baptism are purification from sins and new birth in the Holy Spirit.[37] I finally realized that the sacrament actually accomplishes these things; it is not merely a sign of a decision that one has made to follow Christ. The Catechism goes on:

> Born with a fallen human nature and tainted by original sin, children also have need of the new birth in Baptism to be freed from the power of darkness

---

[37] CCC, paragraph 1262.

and brought into the realm of the freedom of the children of God, to which all men are called. The sheer gratuitousness of the grace of salvation is particularly manifest in infant Baptism. The Church and the parents would deny a child the priceless grace of becoming a child of God were they not to confer Baptism shortly after birth.[38]

Wow! I had denied my children the "priceless grace of becoming a child of God." The Catechism further helped me to understand that infants or children are indeed candidates for Baptism:

> Baptism is the sacrament of faith. But faith needs the community of believers. It is only within the faith of the Church that each of the faithful can believe. *The faith that is required for Baptism is not a perfect and mature faith, but a beginning that is called to develop.*"[39] [Emphasis mine.]

At last, in the summer of 1985, all three of our children were baptized into the Catholic Church in Grand Forks, North Dakota. Praise be to God!

---

[38] Ibid, paragraph 1250.

[39] Ibid, paragraph 1253.

7
On the Move... Again

The years we lived in North Dakota were both enjoyable and fruitful. There was a Couple to Couple League chapter in Grand Forks that we were privileged to join as an NFP teaching couple. One of the other volunteer couples, Phil and Laurie, became life-long friends, and we taught several NFP class series here, with large numbers of students. As our pastor got to know and trust us, he asked us to present at the Pre-Cana weekend events on NFP. There was an abortion clinic in Grand Forks, but the pro-life movement was strong. Ed and I and the kids participated in a "Jericho march" organized by the pro-life group. Hundreds of people marched and prayed around the abortion clinic seven times. Soon that clinic closed, leaving only one abortion clinic in the entire state of North Dakota.

In the fall of 1985, a knock came on our front door. The man who greeted me when I opened the door was either the principal of the local elementary school or the superintendent of schools. (I can't remember which.) After short pleasantries, he said, "I see that you have a five-year-old son who is not enrolled in any of our schools. I'd like to invite you to bring your son to visit your local school." I thanked him and said

7 On the Move...Again

goodbye. All kinds of thoughts swirled through my mind. How did he know we had a five-year old son? Were we going to be persecuted because of our decision to homeschool? Was this visit meant to be a threat? We were aware that the compulsory education laws in North Dakota then were quite strict, only allowing homeschooling if a parent was a certified teacher. When I told Ed about the visitor, he did what he was quite good at: he wrote a letter to this person, politely but firmly informing him that we were homeschooling our son and inviting *him* to visit *our* homeschool. Ed then detailed all the things that Joseph was learning. We didn't receive a reply to this letter, but the man's visit warned us that there could be trouble ahead.

We joined other homeschoolers throughout North Dakota to lobby at the state capital in Bismarck to change the compulsory education laws. We piled all the kids in the Jeep and spent the day along with other families, attending hearings and making our views known to our representatives. We formed good friendships and became acquainted with many North Dakotans. (Due to the sparse population of North Dakota, we felt like we knew nearly everyone who lived there!)

Ed's mother, Mary, living in Grand Rapids, Michigan had been battling cancer for some time and in December 1985, she was nearing death. Ed had not been especially close to his

7   On the Move...Again

mother, but he held her in high esteem. She had, while not being Catholic, been faithful in helping Ed as a child learn the Catholic faith of her husband, Ed's father. We arrived in Michigan a few days before she died, giving us some time to be with her in the hospital, though she was unconscious. She passed away on December 6, 1985 at age 65. My father had graduated after two years in seminary, so Ed asked him to celebrate Mary's funeral as a non-Catholic. (My mother also sang at her funeral.) Mary had willed her house to Ed and had split her estate between her two children, Ed and his older sister, Susan. My parents were in between commitments so it worked out nicely for them to live in Mary's house for the winter, until it could be sold the following spring.

Returning to North Dakota, things were now seen in a different light. Call it wanderlust, call it a desire for adventure, call it looking for perfection, call it running away, call it impulsive...whatever it was, Ed and I were often thinking about moving. (I have a photo of me sitting on the couch in North Dakota with a road atlas open on my lap and a geographic atlas next to me. I remember I was checking out the weather in some state.) He enjoyed his work very much, but we were quite concerned about the strict homeschooling laws in North Dakota. "In the early 1980s, homeschooling was practically unheard of. Even though the model of parents teaching their children at home was one of the earliest (and most effective) forms of education in history, homeschooling had fallen into obscurity. Families who chose such a 'nontraditional' education route often encountered major opposition and legal challenges. Some homeschooling parents were even put in jail for truancy or 'contributing to the delinquency of a minor.' "[40] I like to think that if it hadn't been for this situation with homeschooling that we would have stayed in North Dakota. In many ways, we felt at home there. But some states were more lenient towards homeschooling. Now that we didn't have as much financial pressure, we thought maybe we could go somewhere that allowed parents more freedom.

Poor Mr. Dixon! After only three academic years, Ed turned in his notice that he would be leaving at the end of the school year, the spring of 1987. As a parting shot, Ed wrote a letter to the editor of the Grand Forks Herald explaining why this engineering professor at the university was leaving North Dakota and taking his tax dollars with him. Why? Draconian, antiquated laws against homeschooling.

Where were we going? All we knew is that we were going to Wisconsin, near a small town called Plain. Somehow in our travels we had passed through Plain and visited the Catholic church. There were Stations of the Cross behind the church,

---

[40] "History of HSLDA," Home School Legal Defense Association, www.hslda.org (accessed November 6, 2020).

7 On the Move…Again

which led straight up a steep hill and right through a cow pasture! I followed the Stations and looked out over the stunning view. (Anyone who knows southwest Wisconsin knows how beautiful the fields and hills are there. And to my eyes which had gazed mostly on the Red River Valley of North Dakota for the last three years, it looked like Paradise.) OK, Wisconsin is friendly towards homeschoolers and this is gorgeous and we can go to Mass here; let's move to Wisconsin!

We found a rental farmhouse at the end of a half-mile driveway with two big barns and a lovely creek flowing nearby. The kids were delighted to find a mother cat with several kittens roaming around, and they spent long hours playing in the creek. My parents visited and my mother and I made blackberry jelly from the blackberries that grew profusely up the hill. My old nursing school friend, Pam, and her husband, Drew, and their baby traveled to see us and we went camping together. A time capsule note: this was the first time we rented a video cassette recorder and watched borrowed video tape movies from the library!

Sometime earlier in one of our trips west, we had stopped in Richland Center, Wisconsin and pulled into a Country Kitchen restaurant parking lot. We spotted a bumper sticker from CCL proclaiming something about NFP on one of the cars! We thought we'd better stick around until these people came out of the restaurant so we could meet them. A woman soon emerged and we became acquainted with her, based on our common apostolate of teaching NFP. Her name was Vicki, and she and her family were Wisconsin natives. Fast forward to our current move. We were at the local grocery store when we spotted a lady that looked like Vicki in the parking lot! Yes, it was her, and we told her that we had moved to the area. We resumed our acquaintance and said we'd be in touch. We felt very blessed to have met her again! Little did we know then that Vicki, her husband, Richard, and their family would be involved with our family through thick and thin, through deaths and weddings and births for the next decades.

And now, it seemed good to try to have another baby! Our youngest child, Rachel, was about three years old and financially, we could afford for Ed to take time off from working to care for the children while I became my usual debilitated self with pregnancy. Our Lord graciously gave us His gift of life again! I was relieved that Ed could be home and manage many of our family's needs. We traveled around the area, taking in all the beauty. We dreamed of a future there, and Ed looked at the possibilities for work. Meanwhile, my parents had moved to southern Indiana and were extolling the wonderful aspects of life where they were. I don't know what happened, but it seemed like I wanted to go "home" or to be closer to my parents somehow (which I hadn't really been

7 On the Move...Again

since I married). Long story short, we decided to move to the same town in Indiana where my parents were living.

Early winter, 1987—off we went to Indiana. I had really nailed preparations for moving by this time. I had a list of all the bills, magazines and newspapers, and organizations that needed notification of address changes. The list included things to do and when. It may not have made the physical move any easier, but it relieved stress from my mind! My parents had rented a house for us, a large four-bedroom ranch with a huge yard and perfect tree for hanging up a swing. It was next door to a Protestant church with a paved parking lot, which proved to be just right for Heidi to learn how to ride a bike without training wheels. (That is a favorite memory for me—Heidi wobbling along on her bike, with Joseph prancing along next to her, cheering her on.)

This area was completely new to both Ed and me. We had never lived this far south and we grinned at the southern twang in peoples' speech, the slower pace of life, and the mild winter. We spent that winter thinking about the future...by this time, I was feeling a bit better and Ed was eager to find a job. He looked into applying at Indiana University, which had campuses in many locations in the state of Indiana, as well as Purdue University. We traveled a bit around the area; one of our favorite places to take the kids was Spring Mill State Park, where there was a huge, old grist mill powered by Mill Creek.

7 On the Move...Again

Water flowing from several cave springs led to the founding of an industrial village in the early 1800s. Pioneer entrepreneurs took advantage of a constant water source that never froze, using it to power several gristmills, a wool mill, a saw mill, and a distillery. In turn, pioneer settlers moved in, clearing land for agriculture and timber.[41] Caves, cave boat tours, a pioneer village, and nature center are unique and interesting facets of Spring Mill State Park.

This area was definitely not Catholic as Wisconsin had been. In Wisconsin, there are numerous small Catholic churches scattered all through the countryside. Here in Indiana, the local church we attended was the only Catholic church in the whole county! We met a family there who became friends for some years. This was one of the blessings we enjoyed from living in so many different places. Not only did we learn about the geographical features and the customs and culture of different areas, but we gained valuable friendships, many of which lasted for years. Later when we wanted to travel somewhere, we could think of someone that we could visit just about anywhere!

It was here in Indiana where Ed first learned of the alleged apparitions of our Blessed Mother in Medjugorje. He was fascinated by this and read all he could find about it,

---

[41] "Spring Mill State Park," IN Department of Natural Resources, www.IN.gov (accessed November 10, 2020).

7 On the Move...Again

beginning with a newspaper-like publication by Wayne Weible. I was so busy with home life that I did not read much about it, but I found it interesting that Ed was so caught up in this news. Speaking about home life—maybe this is why we came to Indiana. My mother asked me one day when I was going to begin teaching the children. She didn't mean it in a critical way, but I took offense at the question, thinking I was already teaching them. Based on research in childhood development by Dr. Raymond Moore and his wife, Dorothy, in their book, *Better Late Than Early*, I believed that children (boys in particular) need more time to just be children and not be forced into academic study before age eight or nine.

This does not mean the child is left on his own to do what he wants, however. A daily schedule of activities, with set times for waking and bedtime, meals, and [prayer] is used to provide structure to the child's day. The child participates in helping to care for the family, serving alongside his parents and siblings as they work as a family in the home doing chores...and in community doing service-oriented projects. The parents answer the child's many questions with warm responsiveness and model positive socialization skills and upright moral character.[42]

---

[42] "The Moore Formula," The Home School Mom, www.thehomeschoolmom.com (accessed November 10, 2020).

7   On the Move...Again

Joseph was now almost eight years old and Heidi was five. Heidi had actually begun learning to read, but Joseph still didn't show much inclination towards it. It was time though, and my mother's question was just the kick in the pants I needed. I began formally educating the kids.

Organization and family discipline are not only helpful with homeschooling, I found them to be crucial as we began this more formal phase of home education. Up until this time, I had been more relaxed, incorporating principles of numbers, colors, letters, nature studies, music, poetry, and faith into our everyday life. Thankfully, though, we had started building a solid foundation of loving discipline early on—oh, yes, we had our share of disobedience, sibling squabbling, and other infractions—but overall, we were headed in the right direction. When the Moore's introduced the organizational tip of planning the next week's menu along with a "To Do" list and a "To Buy" list, I was a bit hesitant, but decided to go along with it. This is the tool they suggested:

Take two pieces of 8½" x 11" unlined paper and tape them together end to end. On the top left corner, write "To Do." This is for general obligations needing to be done in no particular time frame. Then write in the seven days of the week across the top of both of the pieces of paper. Back at the left end, in the middle, write the stores where grocery shopping is frequently done, with space underneath to list

7   On the Move...Again

items needed. Moving to the right, divide the area under the days of the week into two or three squares, depending on how many meals need to be planned for each day. (I only made space for two meals, as breakfast didn't really need to be planned in our family.) Leave the bottom area open. Back to the left end again, in the bottom corner, write "To Buy." This space is for non-grocery items. To the right of this, the bottom squares under each day are left open to write in daily chores, either for parents or children. (I did this all by hand every week for many years, but when computers came on the scene, Ed devised a template for me so that I only had to copy it each week.) This became my main organizational tool throughout the 28 years I homeschooled...and I still use it today! It has always been a love/hate relationship—I dread having to do it every Saturday, but I am so thankful for it all week long!

We began preparing earnestly for baby's arrival in late March. I had scheduled another C-section, having given up completely on ever having a natural delivery. My parents were able to be with our three children while we traveled to New Albany, Indiana on March 28, 1988 for the surgery early in the morning of the 29th. While I was waiting to be wheeled into the operating/delivery room, the nurse attending asked me if this was my first child. I told her no, that it is was my fourth. That may have irritated her, or maybe she was merely concerned for my wellbeing when she said, "This is

7 On the Move...Again

dangerous, you know!" It wasn't the most reassuring thought to be left with just before having one's abdomen cut open.

That was the beginning of a difficult delivery, though we were thrilled with our precious new son and thankful for his safe arrival. Vacillating between Lincoln Charles and Charles Lincoln, we decided on the first name of Lincoln. (After all, we were living in Indiana.) But after Lincoln's birth I experienced the worst headache of my life, finding relief only by lying flat on my back. I knew a bit about spinal headaches, that they are caused by leakage of spinal fluid through a puncture hole in the tough membrane (dura mater) that surrounds the spinal cord. This leakage decreases the pressure exerted by the spinal fluid on the brain and spinal cord, which leads to a headache. Sometimes epidural anesthesia may lead to a spinal headache. (I had just had an epidural for the C-section.) Although epidural anesthetic is injected just outside the membrane that surrounds the spinal cord, a spinal headache is possible if the membrane is unintentionally punctured.[43] The anesthesiologist decided to do a "blood patch" repair in an effort to plug the leak. That didn't work, so I spent the first week or so nursing little Lincoln flat on my back and using a bed pan! Poor Ed...he was saddled with many extra duties during those days, but we survived and

---

[43] "Spinal Headaches," Mayo Clinic, www.mayoclinic.org (accessed November 7, 2020).

7 On the Move... Again

rejoiced together as a family for the blessing of Lincoln's arrival.

As much as my life probably surprised my parents, so their life often surprised me. Soon after Lincoln's birth, they decided to move back south to Mississippi. My mother had suffered from poor lung health for much of her life and she said the climate in southern Indiana was not conducive to her well-being. I understood this, but I still felt pain in my heart as it seemed they didn't want to live near my family and me. This feeling of rejection was an incentive for Ed to find work so we could hopefully settle in somewhere. It also made me desire to be closer to Grandma Alice, as she was now in her 80's and I knew her life would be ending in the not-too-distant future. It was difficult for Ed to find another university teaching position, due to his lack of a Ph.D., but we thought of the school where his father had earned his pharmacy degree, Ferris State University (FSU) in Big Rapids, Michigan. This school specialized in more hands-on type degrees, and possibly might be a fit for Ed. It was also only about four hours from Grandma Alice's home.

As he did with UND, Ed called FSU and spoke with someone in the Electrical Engineering Technology department. FSU does not offer an engineering school, but an engineering technology (ET) program. Whereas engineering programs focus on theory and design, ET programs specialize

7 On the Move...Again

in application and implementation. It follows that engineering programs have higher-level math and theoretical science in their curricula, and engineering technology programs tend to put greater emphasis on hands-on laboratory skills.[44] This fact did mesh quite well with Ed's qualifications, and he was offered a faculty position at FSU in late summer 1988. We were on our way back to Michigan!

My good friend, Pam, from nursing school, and her husband, Drew, lived near Grand Rapids so we asked them if they could locate a rental for us quickly. They found a rural house about 20 minutes from FSU, for which the kids were thankful as we told them we could get a dog now. We got the first of several Border Collie dogs, and Rachel named it Jolly. Once we learned we were leaving Indiana, we decided to delay Lincoln's baptism (this again!) until we settled in Michigan. He was baptized at about six months old at Christ the King parish, which was quite close to our new home. While we would not remain parishioners here for long, this parish would feature prominently in my life over the next years.

Ed started work soon after we moved. Most of our possessions remained in boxes in the garage because I was

---

[44] Arnie Peskin, "Engineering vs. Engineering Technology: Who Knows and Who Cares?" www.engineering.com (accessed November 7, 2020).

7 On the Move...Again

hoping we'd find a place to land permanently soon. Ed and I dreamed of building a house—while in Indiana we had drawn up floor plans for a small house—so I searched the newspaper for vacant land for sale. We had fun looking at the available parcels, but one day I saw an ad for a house for sale on land northeast of Big Rapids. We had planned to build, but this piece of real estate looked intriguing.

Both of us fell in love at first sight with this place, which was to be our home together for the next 15 years. It was a chalet-style house with three bedrooms and a finished basement, built on a hillside overlooking a wide, open creek valley and pine forest. The gentle creek burbled along through a maple, oak, and beech woods. A trail led back through the 35 acres, with a neighbor's hunting land behind. It was a half-mile off the county road, with abundant privacy, peace and quiet. The kids loved it too, and we made an offer on it the next day. Beginning in October 1988, this was the place we would call home—where much loving family life, great joy and great sorrow, would occur.

8
Glorifying God in Our Family Life...Sometimes Yes, Sometimes No

It was October and getting cold outside so I had a crash course in learning how to heat with a wood stove; Ed had learned many years ago in Boy Scouts—he was an Eagle Scout—and in Alaska. The former owners had kindly left us a small supply of wood. I gradually learned quite well and grew to love the feel of heat from a wood stove.

Now we could really settle in to homeschooling. You may ask if Michigan had lenient homeschooling laws in 1988. No. It was actually one of the worst states in the country, right along with North Dakota, and families had been greatly victimized. Why in the world had we moved here, when homeschooling-friendly laws were a priority? Ed felt like he had run out of options for work, so his job at FSU trumped everything else. We reasoned that we could move to this remote location, notify no school authorities, and fly under the radar. This was the approach of homeschooling families in those days. We joined the newly-formed Home School Legal Defense Association (HSLDA). Seeing a need for affordable legal advocacy, the founders of HSLDA joined forces in 1983 to establish a nonprofit organization dedicated to protecting families' right to give their children the kind of unique, personalized education that homeschooling allows.[45] For years, I had HSLDA's phone number taped in a prominent place near the phone in the event any authorities came to the front door. The kids were taught what to do in that event, escaping out the back door and running to the neighbor's hunting cabin back in the woods.

It all sounds so dramatic now, but it was a real threat then, as the Mark DeJonge family from Michigan knew all too well. They were charged with violating the compulsory education law in 1984, convicted and sentenced to two years probation, fined $200 each, required to test their children for academic achievement, and ordered to arrange for a certified teacher. They persevered through many court decisions which were not in their favor.[46] This is part of their testimony:

> When we started homeschooling we were very secretive. We did not tell anyone but our parents and some in our small church. When the school bus would go by we would be sure our children were out of sight. Chris [Mrs. DeJonge] was confronted at the

---

[45] "Who We Are," Home School Legal Defense Association, www.hslda.org (accessed November 8, 2020).

[46] "People v. DeJonge," Justia US Law, www.law.justia.com (accessed November 8, 2020).

front door only two weeks into the start of the school year, two or three days after we had received notification that we had been accepted as members in HSLDA. That was a time of anxiety. The social workers were trying to be intimidating as possible and threatened to take away our children because we were not sending our children to school.[47]

Relief didn't come for Michigan homeschoolers and the DeJonge family until 1993, when the Michigan Supreme Court narrowly ruled in their favor and the teacher certification requirement was nullified. This is a fascinating court case that I encourage reading, as it is easy to understand and is refreshing to see the court demolish the lower court rulings and emphasize the great importance of the First Amendment of the U.S. Constitution—the free exercise of religion clause. Simply put, the DeJonge family's case was based on their belief that God gave the responsibility of their children's education exclusively to them, not the state. Therefore it was a free exercise of religion case. It did not affect compulsory education laws...[48]

---

[47] "Mark and Christine DeJonge—History of Homeschooling in Michigan," Michigan Christian Homeschool Network, www.michn.org (accessed November 8, 2020).

[48] "American Educational History: A Hypertext Timeline," www.eds-resources.com (accessed November 12, 2020).

8   Glorifying God in our Family Life—Sometimes Yes, Sometimes No

When we began homeschooling there were few curricula providers, but as the movement grew, so did the options. Various methods included something called "unschooling," the classical method, the Charlotte Mason method, the unit study method, Montessori, Waldorf/Steiner, traditional, and more. I was interested in learning some of these various methods and often mixed and matched them. In the beginning with young children, some simple books were enormously helpful: *A Strong Start in Language, A Home Start in Reading,* and *An Easy Start in Arithmetic,* all by Ruth Beechick. In the early years, there were few Catholic sources of teaching materials. We resorted to using Protestant and secular books, but were careful to edit objectionable material and supplement with information from Catholic reference books. About 10 years into our homeschooling adventures, I finally settled on a classical curriculum with the help of Laura Berquist's *Designing Your Own Classical Curriculum.* A faithful Catholic, Laura went on to found Our Lady of Divine Grace homeschool program to assist parents in providing a classical education for their children. There are other faithful Catholic providers as well, including Seton Home Study School, Kolbe Academy, Our Lady of Victory and others.

Sometimes curriculum wasn't needed at all. When Joseph was about 10 or 11, he had turned in a paper for a writing assignment that was pretty nearly copied word for word from

8   Glorifying God in our Family Life—Sometimes Yes, Sometimes No

the encyclopedia. As I read it, I sighed and said, "We have *got* to do something about Joseph's writing!" I presented the problem to Ed, a teacher par excellence. After thinking about it for a time, he suggested that Joseph choose a topic from the encyclopedia (World Book Encyclopedias were great in those days!) and read a sentence or two. Then he was to close the book and write in his own words what he had just read. After doing this for a day or two, the length of the selection was to be increased repeatedly until after a week or so, he would be writing nearly a paragraph after closing the book. (It was helpful if the topic was something Joseph was interested in.) This forced him to formulate thoughts in his own words without copying them—the essence of writing. It worked remarkably well. (Thirty years later, Joseph's first book was published.) Ed had a gift of seeing the big picture of an idea and how to break that down into the necessary elements to learn it.

We were eager to put down roots and begin building our little homestead. The menagerie started out with the aforementioned dog, Jolly, a cat named Kitty, and a rabbit, Gentle. Based on my memories of participating in 4-H as a child (my brothers and I had shown dairy cattle at the county fair), I inquired about a 4-H club. I found the best rabbit club leader just a few miles away! This was the start of many years in 4-H for our family, showing rabbits and pigs and entering various exhibits. The kids have fond memories—and some stressful ones—from their 4-H experiences! Until it was time to butcher the pigs, we all enjoyed companionship with, and the funny antics of, the animals. Showing a pig at the 4-H fair includes walking the pig around an arena with a cane to guide the pig. So when we took family walks around our "farmette," we turned the pigs loose and they followed us down the lane and around the pasture while the kids practiced their skills with the cane. We eventually added milking goats and a horse to our animal collection. The goats would follow us around too—they were very funny—and the animals were all friends! The dog and the horse would often visit the pigs; I guess they were the center of attraction to the other animals!

Family life revolved around Ed's teaching at the university, my work homemaking and educating the kids, and the kids' learning how to become responsible, faithful adults. This involved play of course. Ed often got down on the floor on all fours and let the small children crawl all over him like a mini jungle gym. The children roamed in the woods close to home and built forts out of branches. There was a tire swing on a tree branch there too. We shared many projects—one was a homemade bread baking business. Each of the older children had a particular type of bread that was their responsibility: whole wheat, white, or French. One child kept the "financial records" and one child washed the dishes and cleaned up. Ed brought many loaves to work with him every week for a donation from his co-workers.

Another favorite memory I have is of the three older children climbing in the plum tree in the yard as I gazed out the window at them having so much fun. It was one of those bittersweet times when all seems right with the world and there is peace in one's heart, but as I realized then, "It will not always be this way. Trouble will come one day; soak in this moment." Earthly life with all its beauty is fragile and passing away.

Chores began early in our young ones' lives. When Lincoln was five years old, Grandma Alice was visiting. It was Lincoln's turn to wash the breakfast dishes—we never did use the dishwasher—and he was procrastinating and whining about it as he stood on a stool at the sink. Grandma Alice looked at me with a wistful look and said, "Oh, he's just a baby!" So she helped him get started and gave him encouragement along the way. We laugh about her comment now when we want to tease Lincoln about something.

We searched out homeschooling friends for the kids. There were no Catholics homeschooling in our area then, and few in the whole nation. In 1983, the newly-created Seton Home Study School boasted only 50 students.[49] So we formed

---

[49] "Seton's History," Seton Home Study School, www.setonhome.org (accessed November 12, 2020).

a local homeschool group with several Protestant families who became good friends. We held science fairs, baseball games, baking days, and work bees. For baking days, the moms would gather at one family's home and make 10 or 15 pies for the freezer, for example. Then we'd do something similar at another family's home. Work bees were very interesting. Each family would plan a major project that required some extensive labor. I remember wallpapering one family's home, including stairwells! I also wrote and mailed out a newsletter to keep everyone informed. Our families relied on each other for friendship, advice, understanding. It was a very important community for our family.

Sadly, our local Catholic parish was not an important community for our family. We tried very hard to fit in, sending some of the kids to the religious education program, even though we taught the Faith at home. The pastor was one of the few who was supportive of NFP and referred couples to us for classes. This, though, set us apart as the ones who didn't go along with contraception...as if we were right-wing extremists. In addition, we didn't support the parish school by sending our kids there...and even worse, we homeschooled! We felt like outcasts, and the only friendship we gained there was with a family who had just moved to the area. Their son was about Rachel's age and they were in the First Communion class together. The mother, Debbie, was intrigued with

8 Glorifying God in our Family Life—Sometimes Yes, Sometimes No

homeschooling and asked me to come to her house and talk about it. She was convinced that's what she wanted to do for her two children. Though this family moved away not too much later, our families became dear friends, and Debbie was to play a very important part in my personal life years later.

It was the summer of 1990 that my father's anti-Catholicism met head on with my husband. Ed, as a teacher, had the summer months off so we drove down to Mississippi to visit my parents. They were working at a Bible camp, but there were no campers there when we visited. One day, the kids and I were riding in the car with my parents. Dad frequently talked about the need to be saved, and how important a personal relationship with Jesus is, especially directed to our children. That day, to my shame, I took offense at this, feeling like he was directly challenging our faith and confusing our children. I seethed inside. Though I said nothing about it in the car, that night when Ed and I had gone to bed, about 9 PM or so, I told him about it and expressed my anger. He and I and baby Lincoln were staying in one of the campers' dorms, while the three older kids were at Mom and Dad's house just up the road. Ed got out of bed, put on his clothes, and went up to their house. What happened there I only know from what Ed and the older kids told me later. He must have been very angry, which was totally out of character for him.

8 Glorifying God in our Family Life—Sometimes Yes, Sometimes No

There was written material at Mom and Dad's house that was anti-Catholic. That, plus the comments to me in the car about our children needing to be saved, was too much for Ed; my father seemed to consider our children as non-Christians while he was the "right" example of Christianity. Ed never told me what he said or exactly what happened, but the kids said it was terrible to hear as they lay in bed.

The next morning, Mom was waiting outside the dorm building for us, crying. I was ashamed at my part in this, yet I was somewhat gratified that Ed had set boundaries. I sat down next to Mom and we cried together. That afternoon, Ed went with Dad to town and apologized to him. I don't know what was said then either, but Ed assured me he was remorseful and had given a sincere apology. Dad too, wrote a heartfelt letter of apology to Ed and me later. He was quite sorry that what he had said offended us.

The relationship between my father and my husband never really recovered from that altercation. It hurt my father terribly; a year or two later when they were visiting us, he said to me that he had never had anyone speak to him that way. I could tell it still hurt him. I don't know if he was able to forgive Ed or not. True to my father's character however, years later when I needed my parents so much, he was there for me.

I have thought long and hard about my responsibility for this ruptured relationship. It stems from the power we women have, which we may or may not realize. I think men are wired to protect, to serve, to fix problems. As a wife, if I complain or express anger or indignation to my husband, he will naturally want to do something about it. I have the power to influence his emotions to a great extent as well. This can be put to great advantage, but it also has the potential for great harm.

We tried to live the Catholic faith in our family with the hope of growing in humility and kindness. I rekindled my love for the elderly, stemming from my work at the nursing home as a teen, so the kids and I made regular excursions to our local nursing home to visit. We went to a friend's house weekly for nearly two years to help her care for her elderly father until he passed away.

Ed and I brought the good news of NFP to the public with a Couple to Couple League (CCL) information booth at the area health fair, where we met two Protestant ladies one day. (All the years we lived here, we taught NFP to more Protestant couples than Catholic couples!) They were interested not only in NFP, but in homeschooling, so they came to our house and spent a day with us just to see how we lived our life. They later organized a homeschooling information day for area Protestant families and asked me to be a speaker. I was privileged to share our family's story, and

8 Glorifying God in our Family Life—Sometimes Yes, Sometimes No

Heidi and Rachel got to earn some money as babysitters. One of these ladies and her husband took our NFP class. They said they planned not to have any children. After the class, they went on to have several children and even to adopt! I always thought of their story as a real success for NFP. God opens hearts to life!

Our hearts were opened again too, and in 1992 I became pregnant with baby number five. The old familiar nausea returned. Several of our Protestant homeschooling moms were having babies and invited me to be present at their births at home with a midwife. What an honor and a privilege it was for me to share these intimate moments of beautiful natural childbirth with our friends! One of these women said to me, "You could have a home birth too." I said, "After four C-sections?! I don't think so!" Nevertheless, the idea was planted in my mind and I ever so carefully tiptoed into exploring natural childbirth at home. I met with the same midwife, Patrice, who'd delivered my friends' babies. She was very knowledgeable and experienced, and after reviewing my medical records, echoed what my friend had said. She thought it was possible. I was not so sure, but I did have several check-ups with Patrice. One day when I was ten weeks pregnant, the nausea left me and I thought, "Oh, what a relief...it's gone earlier this time." But then I started bleeding, which had never happened in previous pregnancies. I called

Patrice who counseled me on what to do and what to watch for, but God did not allow us to meet this little person. The miscarriage of our child, whom we named MaryLeah, was followed by a D&C at the local hospital. (Mary was for Ed's mother and Leah for his paternal grandmother, whose prayers Ed said were the reason he was still Catholic.) There is great consolation now to think of MaryLeah in heaven and to anticipate meeting her one day, but the grief and sadness were overwhelming when I went to the obstetrician's office for a check-up after the D&C and saw all the pregnant mothers and newborns...but life was so busy and I needed to go on.

There were always new adventures. The Couple to Couple League typically held national conventions every two years to bring together NFP families, teachers and promoters. In 1992, the convention was coming to Grand Rapids. We were good friends with the CCL chapter members in Grand Rapids and were asked to assist in planning the convention. God seemed to throw me into these preparations, knowing they would lay the groundwork for His plans for me later on in furthering His kingdom. I was put in charge of numerous NFP theologians and experts who were scheduled as speakers. I was definitely out of my league and in over my head, but I couldn't back out now. I was to arrange all their travel plans and make sure all their needs were met at the convention. Ed was in charge of transportation for all the speakers, keeping track of their

8 Glorifying God in our Family Life—Sometimes Yes, Sometimes No

arrival and departure times from the airport. I also had the opportunity to plan a schedule, organize, and invite many workshop speakers who would present throughout the four-day convention. There were workshops on home businesses, homeschooling, health concerns, spirituality, and several other topics. From our travels over the years, I knew people who had expertise in various fields and most of them graciously accepted the invitation to speak at the conference. Organizing all these speakers and workshops definitely stretched my abilities and caused me to grow. So Ed took this opportunity to propose the purchase of our first desktop computer! He had been campaigning for this for some time, as he had been working with computers at the university, but I was still happy with my Selectric typewriter. I finally relented, and the Stuarts joined the computer age in 1992. (It *was* a big help with the convention!)

1993 was the year that our beloved Pope St. John Paul II came to Denver. Ed took Joseph, who was 13, with him and they traveled out to Cherry Creek State Park to spend time with our Holy Father. What a blessed trip they had! And while they were away, the ladies were up to something at home. Heidi and Rachel had asked about owning their very own horse for quite some time, as many young girls do. I did too as a young girl. But we had no extra money for luxuries then on my parents' dairy farm, so I could only dream of horses and ride occasionally at friends' houses. I now thought it was time to make the dreams of three of us come true. The girls saw an ad in the paper for a horse for sale. I knew nothing of how to buy a horse, so I asked one of our homeschooling moms who did know to come with us. The first horse we looked at was not acceptable, but the second one...oh, he was beautiful! He was a chestnut quarter horse with a white stripe down the middle of his face. He had been a barrel racer but was retired now, and was just old enough to be less rambunctious for the kids, but with enough zip to be fun. I wanted to get a fence up before Ed got home so that he wouldn't have to do it, so I asked my brother, Randy, to help me. He drove four hours to our house and together we installed the electric fence all around the pasture for the horse, named Vandy.

What a surprise for Ed and Joseph! I don't think I could keep it secret though; when Ed called me from a motel somewhere, I broke the news to him. He took it in stride, without saying too much. I will always remember the first time the kids and I enjoyed leading and riding Vandy around, taking turns for each child. I promised Ed that I would take care of the horse and it wouldn't be any extra work for him...until I asked for a horse barn! He was not a carpenter, but he loved to learn new things, so sure enough—he built it!

It was a busy summer for Ed. This was the year he finally got to fulfill his dream of traveling to Medjugorje, the site of the alleged ongoing appearances of the Blessed Mother to six young people. We had attended a Marian conference for several years in northern Michigan; the woman who was the driving force behind the conference was a real fireball of love for Mary. She led a pilgrimage group to this simple village in eastern Europe, and Ed went with them. As might be expected, it was a life-changing experience for him, and eventually for our family. As Ed's devotion to Mary grew he suggested, with trepidation, that we try to pray the rosary as a family. (He remembered my reaction to the rosary years before at the first retreat I attended!) I was hesitant but agreed, so we started praying the rosary intermittently in the evenings together. We got little prayer booklets with pictures of each mystery to help the children understand and follow along. Ed even convinced me to try fasting on bread and water on Wednesdays and Fridays. This we did too as a family for a time, but we just couldn't sustain that for long. These practices may sound like superficial, empty works, not pleasing to God. But they began to have effects in my soul, as the most holy and lovable Mother of God found a crack in my armor and moved in. Our spiritual growth sometimes occurs in fits and starts; some experience causes our spirits to soar to heaven and we engross ourselves in Scripture or good works or prayer. And then we may stagnate for a time, which carries with it the danger of falling away from our "first love." Ed's trip to Medjugorje was the inspiration for me to begin again, to refresh my spiritual life with the intercession of our Blessed Mother.

Our desire for Catholic rural community had not gone away, though we loved our place and didn't really want to move (surprising, eh?). I just thought I'd put out some feelers, so I wrote a letter to a magazine begun in 1991 called *Caelum et Terra* (Heaven and Earth). The magazine published articles on homeschooling, family prayer and ritual, gardening, cooperative enterprise, and other very down-to-earth matters. The founders believed that

> ...agriculture is the best and most natural foundation for a Christian society. [They] showed a deep interest in the agrarianism [a perspective that stresses the primacy of family farming, widespread property ownership, and political decentralization][50] which was prophetically recommended by Catholic and other thinkers in the earlier part of the [last] century and which re-emerged as a conscious and practicing movement in the 1960s. At the same time, the founders believed that a well-ordered commonwealth

---

[50] *Britannica Encyclopedia*, s.v. "Agrarianism," www.britannica.com (accessed November 12, 2020).

includes both town and country and explored means of humanizing city life.⁵¹

This was right up our alley. We soon heard from a young man whose parents lived about an hour away from us on a small homestead. They had a large family and as we got acquainted with each other, they introduced us to other families of like mind in their area. We formed valuable friendships and supported each other in our Catholic faith and homesteading efforts, traveling to visit each other once or twice a month. We were delighted to experience this fellowship.

The situation at our local parish was deteriorating. The faithful, NFP-promoting priest was transferred to another parish and the new pastor was not supportive of our efforts. Other nearby parishes were suffering too. As an example, in our deanery, (a small geographical grouping of parishes under the care of a priest "dean," or leader) three of ten priests had left the priesthood after the fallout from the sex scandals in the early 2000's. Spiritual leadership and formation of the faithful seemed to be lacking, so we began traveling an hour or so to more distant parishes every Sunday for Mass. This became a

---

[51] Maclin and Karen Horton and Daniel Nichols, "Why *Caelum et Terra?*" www.caelumetterra.wordpress.com (accessed November 11, 2020).

"pilgrimage" for our family, as we'd have time in the car to pray the rosary and talk about the Mass. However, it led to difficulties in procuring the sacraments for our children, such as First Reconciliation and Communion and Confirmation. Not only were we not registered parishioners at any parish, we homeschooled and didn't generally send our children to faith formation programs. God always provided though; our children received sacraments in at least seven different parishes, with one Confirmation in South Dakota and one Confirmation in Detroit!

One of these parishes we traveled to was Christ the King, the same parish we had originally attended when we moved back to Michigan and in which Lincoln had been baptized. We would go to Mass there sporadically; one Sunday Ed leaned over and whispered in my ear, "Look over to the far right, about halfway back. Do you see someone you recognize?" I gasped...it was his sister, Susan, who had left the Catholic Church to elope with her husband, Jack, many years before. There she was with Jack, who had been a Lutheran the last we knew. We hurried to greet them after Mass and learned of how God worked through their neighbor to bring, first Jack to RCIA (Rite of Christian Initiation of Adults), then Susan. Ed considered this quite miraculous—not only their conversions, but that they would be at this parish and we would see them! We had not had much of a relationship with Jack and Sue since we married, but this was the beginning of a welcomed connection with them.

Promoting homeschooling was very important to me, and I was distressed at the lack of interest among Catholics. I met a woman who shared the desire to promote it amongst Catholics—though we never met face to face, but only talked on the phone—and we decided to start a Catholic homeschooling magazine. The next months were intense. I called on all the friends we had met throughout the country, some of whom were now homeschooling, to assist in writing articles and offering advice. (Our magazine was the first to publish my review of *Designing Your Own Catholic Curriculum* by Laura Berquist.) It was a crash course in publishing and our first issue of *Catholic Family's Magnificat!* came out in June 1994.

We were both determined women with strong opinions. We worked well together as we assembled the first issue and planned subsequent ones. But just before the premiere issue went to the printer, I found several errors that I wanted to be corrected. She had made the arrangements with the printer and didn't want to postpone printing any longer. She didn't budge, and neither did I. I asked her to remove my name from the editorial page, as I did not want to be associated with a publication containing these errors. Much to her credit, she continued with the publication of this periodical for several more issues, then kept it afloat on the internet for some time. We parted on good terms and corresponded for the next year or two. I think the kids were thankful that my publishing career was short-lived!

9
Pray Always

1995 and I was pregnant again! We were overjoyed! Lincoln was now seven years old; he would be a good big brother and Heidi, in particular, had prayed for a baby. We all missed the presence of an infant. Additionally, Ed was nearly 48 and I was 37...it seemed like now or never. The girls were old enough to help with cooking; eating frequently eased my nausea, so they kept busy making things that I could eat. And I couldn't stop thinking about home birth. Such an intriguing idea, that even I might be a candidate for this. The midwife, Patrice, seemed undaunted by the fact I had had four C-sections, but...well, I needed to find out some facts for myself.

I need to emphasize here that this was my personal experience and I do not intend to recommend that anyone else follow my birth plan. Everyone should consult with their own health provider to determine their birthing options. I began with books that Patrice loaned to me: *Spiritual Midwifery* by Ina May Gaskin, *Homebirth: The Essential Guide to Giving Birth Outside of the Hospital* by Sheila Kitzinger, *A Good Birth, A Safe Birth: Choosing and Having the Childbirth Experience You Want* by Diana Korte. Then I did additional research, particularly for information on the complications that could occur with home birth specifically after C-sections. At that time, there was a trend toward more VBAC (vaginal birth after cesarean) deliveries. Though this trend reversed in subsequent years, it was strong in 1995.

I discovered two dangerous complications of VBAC that seemed to pertain particularly to me: uterine rupture and placenta previa. Uterine rupture affects about one percent of women who attempt VBAC. While rare, it means the uterus tears open during labor, usually along the previous C-section scar, and may require an emergency C-section.[52] Placenta previa means that the placenta lies low in the uterus and partially or completely covers the cervix, leading to bleeding and potential blockage of the baby's delivery during labor. It affects about one in 200 pregnant women but is more common in women who've had more than one child and who've had C-sections.[53] I also learned that the more C-sections a woman has had, the higher the risk for placenta previa. I discussed these complications, and others, with Patrice. She reassured me that she and her apprentice midwife, Laurie, were familiar

---

[52] "Home Birth After Cesarean (HBAC): What You Need to Know," healthline Parenthood, www.healthline.com (accessed November 12, 2020).

[53] "Placenta Previa," American Pregnancy Association, www.americanpregnancy.org (accessed November 12, 2020).

9 Pray Always

with what to watch for and had strategies to overcome the complications. Also she assured me she would always be observant about when to seek medical care.

I felt confident about her knowledge and advice (she had specific guidelines on diet and exercise, for example, specifying that I walk a mile every day), but I also took steps on my own to increase my chances for a successful, healthy delivery, e.g., I visited the local obstetrician regularly and requested an ultrasound near the end of my pregnancy to ascertain that the placenta was in the correct position. I even called Dr. Mayer Eisenstein, an obstetrician practicing near Chicago who specialized in home births. He was willing to take me as a patient, but I would have to deliver there and I decided that was a bit too far to travel...and wouldn't be home! Through my entire pregnancy, I read, read, read: textbooks, articles, and many birth stories. Ed said that I earned a Ph.D. in natural childbirth by the time it was over!

Certain saints became very close to me too. I've heard it described that pregnancy and labor make the veil between heaven and earth quite thin indeed. Prayers to my favorites asking for their intercession were nearly continuous: St. Gerard, St. Thomas More, St. Philomena, and our Blessed Mother. (When I read that St. Thomas More would stop whatever he was doing and pray whenever one of the women in his large household was laboring to deliver a baby, I knew I

9 Pray Always

wanted him praying for me too!) The thought of "praying" to saints may strike some as idolatrous or just plain wrong, but Catholics do not worship saints or expect them to have the power of God. The prayers to saints are simply asking them to pray for us *to God,* just as here on earth one may ask a friend to pray for one's needs. "The prayer of the righteous is powerful and effective" (James 5:16). The saints are closer to God than any of us here on earth!

Why did I desire to attempt this home birth? Why was I not content to just plan another C-section delivery? I was very thankful for medical assistance and for healthy babies, but I remembered the Demerol, the x-ray, the uterine infection, the general anesthesia, the spinal headache, and especially the separation from my babies of the first four deliveries and I contrasted that with the beauty of the several home births I had witnessed. I do, however, acknowledge that there are women who desire the assurance of the latest medical technology nearby when they give birth. This medical care is truly life-saving in some cases, and I am thankful that it is available.

As I studied home birth I learned: the incidence of infection is lower, fewer medical interventions lead to greater success in natural deliveries, and there is increased opportunity for baby/mother bonding. I was amazed to hear Patrice's stories of the many births she had attended and all the complications she had successfully dealt with. I was thoroughly convinced that she could help me deliver a baby naturally in situations that some physicians are not experienced in or may not be confident in...and may not want to take the time for. For example, an episiotomy, which the American Heritage Dictionary defines as a surgical incision of the perineum during childbirth to facilitate delivery, is being performed in many hospitals in rates from 20-40 percent of deliveries.[54] This same study reported that "a leading hospital safety group recommends that the cuts should occur in no more than 5% of vaginal deliveries."[55] A midwife knows how to assist, and takes the time to allow, the woman's body to make way for the baby. An episiotomy is less likely to occur when the woman is cared for by a midwife who is known and trusted. This trust was a major factor for me—I trusted Patrice completely to not only help me achieve a successful natural birth, but to do it safely.

Meanwhile, we were still interested in Catholic community. We had come to know Father Robert Fox from Alexandria, South Dakota, who hosted an annual Marian Congress (conference) in that small town and where the

---

[54] Tracy Clark-Flory, "Hospitals are Performing Episiotomies Way Too Often, Despite Decades of Warnings," Jezebel, www.jezebel.com (accessed November 13, 2020).

[55] Ibid.

9 Pray Always

Fatima Family Shrine is located. Families were moving to Alexandria to be near each other in a faithful Catholic environment. (The beautiful parish church, St. Mary of Mercy, has a very moving, realistic crucifix above the Tabernacle. It's a quiet, prayerful place to visit.) In the summer of 1995, while I was pregnant, we packed up and moved to Alexandria for the summer months during which Ed was not teaching. It was another Beverly Hillbilly scene—unlike the pickup we drove when moving to Alaska, this time it was a woody station wagon with kids buckled in everywhere, while the dog and I were lying together in the very back as I was, yes...sick as a dog. The car bottomed out frequently from all the boxes and from pulling the U-Haul trailer behind it. It was to be a trial run to see if God might be calling us to move to Alexandria. We rented a small house in town and the kids thought it was great to ride their bikes all over, to the post office, the store, to church. Father Fox was wonderful, and more valuable friendships developed. (One of the families we befriended had a young daughter who grew up to have a best friend who is now my daughter-in-law.)

One of the highlights of our stay there was the visit of the alleged stigmatist, "Francis." (A stigmatist is a person believed to be supernaturally marked with wounds resembling those of the crucified Christ.) Father Fox had come to learn of this man (who went by the name of Francis for the sake of

9 Pray Always

anonymity) from the Upper Peninsula of Michigan. Father invited him to come to the Marian Congress that year, the same summer we lived in Alexandria, and Father personally witnessed what he described as the Passion of Christ being lived out in Francis. He went on to become the spiritual advisor for Francis, and wrote a detailed book about him. The phenomenon had begun on Good Friday in 1993 and was repeated every night between midnight and 3 AM "to save sinners and to touch God's children. His entire suffering was for the conversion of sinners."[56] Many alleged miracles have occurred from Francis' public ministry which lasted until his death in 2009: to touch and to pray over people. Our family was privileged to participate in a healing service after Mass one evening in Alexandria and it was especially powerful for me. I was about four months pregnant and considering a radical departure from standard medical procedure for the birth of my baby. When I stood in front of Francis, he lightly placed his hands, with the apparent marks of the stigmata on them, on my head and asked me if I was pregnant. When I replied I was, he paused as if praying and said, "You will have a nice baby!" I wasn't sure what "nice" meant, but it seemed positive; I hadn't asked him about my pregnancy or even said

---

[56] Eddie O'Neill, "Michigan Stigmatic on Path Toward Sainthood," Our Sunday Visitor, www.osvnews.com (accessed November 14, 2020).

9   Pray Always

a word to him, yet after prayer, he assured me about this upcoming important event in my life. What a consolation! The tabernacle containing the Blessed Sacrament was off to the side of the church at that time (it has since been moved back to the center) and I went over and knelt in front of Jesus and prayed prayers of thanksgiving.

Those were beautiful months in Alexandria, but the lack of adequate employment for Ed brought us back to Michigan. My love for our home had not waned, so I was not unhappy. We set about making proximate preparations for the birth of our baby. As the children were older now (15, 12 ½, 11, and 7 ½), they joined Ed in taking care of me. I felt their love very much as this body, which felt very old, grew clumsy and increasingly pained. Though they were involved in school and outside activities, they found time for household chores and cooking. As baby's due date was in the winter, some good friends arranged with midwife Patrice to lend her their Suburban so she could make it in our driveway in the event it was drifted and Ed was busy with my labor. (It was an overwhelming task of clearing that half-mile driveway of snow every winter! I often said it seemed *designed* to drift full of snow. At times we parked a vehicle at the end of it, near the road, and trekked in and out through the drifts, kids and groceries in hand.) We had lined up many people to pray, ordered hygienic supplies, and awaited the big day. Labor

9 Pray Always

began on the last day of November in the middle of the night. God timed it perfectly! It was Thursday night and the contractions were mild, so Ed went to work on Friday while I rested on an air mattress in the living room all day. The kids rubbed my back and generally attended to my needs. When Ed arrived home that evening, I decided to take a bath. That really intensified the contractions and in panic I told Ed he'd better call the midwife and then read the instructions on how to deliver a baby! He retorted that I'd better figure out if this was the real thing or not. We laughed together, as neither of us had been through this whole process before. The midwives arrived and assured us everything was as it should be. At a difficult point in the labor, I realized that though I had prepared to the best of my ability, it wouldn't be me who birthed this baby, but the power of God. I surrendered completely to Him and quit trying to control the pain, the positions, the sounds...everything. That's when He took over and it was soon time for our child's birth.

All went well until the baby's shoulders became stuck—one of those uncommon complications called shoulder dystocia. Patrice had mentioned this in one of our pre-natal visits but I had not paid too much attention to it. I paid attention now! She said sharply, "Fae, get up on your hands and knees right now! Ed, lie underneath her upper body to raise her up!" There was palpable tension in the air and it took

9 Pray Always

all I had to soldier on, but then the glorious moment came when I felt the rest of our son's body be born. It was 4:45 AM, December 2, 1995. My first child, Joseph, weighed 8 pounds, 8 ounces at birth. My medical records from his birth stated that the reason for the first C-section was failure to progress and CPD (cephalopelvic disproportion). This means that the baby's head or body is too large to fit through the mother's pelvis. Yet with the right amount of time and patience from the midwives, my youngest child, weighing 9 pounds, 5 ounces was birthed naturally at home. I praise God for this gift!

Baby Boy Stuart went without a name for nearly two weeks. We decided to involve the kids in the decision-making process and that was interesting! We had lists of names and we all voted on them. That didn't get us very far. Then my Aunt Arlene, my father's only sister, came to help care for our family—she was a great cook—and she chimed in with her favorite names. We were still at an impasse. We have had the long tradition of reading out loud to the kids in the evenings ever since Joseph was born and we had been reading a book called *Black Fox of Lorne*. The young hero was called John, Jan, or Ian depending on which European country he happened to be in. One night the name Ian just jumped out at me and I asked Ed if he liked it. He did, and that finally settled the first name. His full name is Ian Edward Campion

9 Pray Always

Stuart. Edward is for his father and Campion is for St. Edmund Campion, a heroic priest-martyr whom we had just read about as well. Ian missed being born on his feast day of December 1 by just a few hours.

What a joy it was to revel in the miracle of his birth, to snuggle him close, and to enjoy our whole family together. Heidi made homemade cinnamon rolls that morning and shared with the midwives; it was such a festive atmosphere. Later that morning, Ed was so tired he crawled under a desk in the office and slept on the floor for awhile...our bed wasn't available...Ian and I were getting to know each other.

Life with a new baby was joyful and challenging and God continued to challenge me in my spiritual life too. A short comment from a friend made a drastic difference in my life. We were talking on the phone when she asked me if I prayed every day. I had to answer no. Even though we were faithfully praying the rosary, I didn't pray privately every day in intimate communion with God. She said, "You can't expect to grow in holiness if you aren't praying every day." I desired very much to grow in holiness, so I took her advice to heart. The priest at one of the parishes we were attending described in a homily one Sunday a method of prayer that I latched on to: a prayer journal in which one writes prayers of praise and thanksgiving, then prayers for other people, then for oneself. It is a simple tool that can be minimized or expanded as

9 Pray Always

desired, and I have kept this prayer journal now for many years. The important thing is that prayer arise from one's heart to God in love.

> If you sometimes find yourself so troubled and disturbed that you cannot find peace, turn immediately to prayer and persevere in it....[Even though] you feel saddened and faint-hearted, you must not distance yourself from prayer, until your will is conformed to God's, and, consequently, is fervent and peaceful and at the same time entirely quickened and undaunted in order to accept and embrace what you formerly feared and abhorred.[57]

We were still traveling nearly an hour and a half to attend Mass, but we had also gotten to be friends with some of the local parishioners. We decided to form a group that would meet weekly to study apologetics. Apologetics comes from the Greek word *apologia* meaning a "defense." In his first letter, St. Peter says, "Always be ready to give an explanation to anyone who asks you a reason for your hope" (1 Peter 3:15). Catholic apologetics, specifically, is the defense and explanation of the teachings, beliefs, and practices of the

---

[57] Blessed Clelia Merloni, "A House of Prayer." *Magnificat* Vol. 22, No. 9 (2020): 299.

Catholic Church.[58] We called our little group, *Why be Catholic?* and met at the home of one of our friends. News spread by word of mouth and with ads in the local newspaper. This proved to be so successful that we moved the venue to the local hospital meeting room. Ed and I had become the informal leaders of the group and prepared written lesson plans for each meeting. Topics discussed included papal authority, the relationship of faith and works in salvation, the Eucharist (Holy Communion), questions about Mary's role, the sacraments, and several others. Ed even devised a *Bible Quiz for Bible Christians* for friends and family members. (See Appendix 2.) We were learning the Faith a bit more formally too, by working on Father John Hardon's *Basic Catholic Catechist's Course* by mail. We were eventually certified as satisfactorily completing that course.

God seemed to place in our hearts a desire to study and share the Catholic Faith with others. This must have been one way He was strengthening my own faith. In an email from Thomas J. McKenna, the founder and president of Catholic Action for Faith and Family, he discusses the theological virtue of faith:

---

[58] Will Wright, "Catholic Apologetics: A How-To Guide To Defending the Faith," Catholic-Link, www.catholiclink.org (accessed November 15, 2020).

9 Pray Always

Faith is rooted in the mind and is an intellectual assent to what God has revealed. The mind accepts God's existence as true and gives credence to the Word He pronounces (through scripture and doctrine), even though we might not fully understand everything that is revealed. St. Anselm said that theology (which includes our basic learning of the catechism) is "Faith seeking understanding." Faith does not require a full understanding of everything that God has revealed. It is simply the acknowledgement of God and His Word as true.

But this is also why faith demands regular study. C.S. Lewis says in *Mere Christianity* that "we have to be continuously reminded of what we believe." Even though faith is a gift of God, it is a gift that grows with our efforts to understand the things of God and His will for our lives.

Faith is also a creative force in the world. Those who offer their gifts back to God in service of others often have a positive impact on the world that far outweighs even their own natural gifts. They simply need to acknowledge the sovereignty of God over everything they do—and then offer it all back to Him. The Catechism says that "the disciple of Christ must not only keep the Faith and live on it, but also

9 Pray Always

profess it, confidently bear witness to it, and spread it." (*CCC*, 1816). Faith must be shared if it is to change the world.[59]

This is what our *Why Be Catholic?* group tried to do. The *Catechism of the Catholic Church* had recently been published and a powerful preacher appeared on EWTN (Eternal Word Television Network), and around the nation. He recorded a lengthy teaching series on the Catechism called *The Teaching of Jesus Christ*, 50 hour-long lectures explaining it in great detail. Our *Why Be Catholic?* group wanted to host this series at a local parish, but one of the priests told us that the Catechism wasn't meant for the laity to study, but only the bishops. That didn't make sense to us, as the Catechism itself said it was for all the faithful. We went ahead and hosted this entire series at the hospital every week for over a year, writing up review questions for the attendees to discuss after viewing the video. This was a convenient class for our older children to study the Catechism too.

When that series ended we moved into Christopher West's presentations on Pope St. John Paul II's *Theology of the Body* teachings. From 1979 to 1984, the Pope gave 129 weekly

---

[59] Thomas J. McKenna, Catholic Action for Faith and Family, www.catholicaction.org/ (accessed October 8, 2020). Used with permission.

talks on human sexuality and marriage. The "theology of the body" refers to the study of who God is and who we are by reflecting on what God has revealed about the human body, especially in the context of Christian marriage.[60] In subsequent years, this theology would be fleshed out by numerous marriage and family scholars. This, in turn, would light the way to help parents form their children in Catholic identity, healthy relationships, purity, dating/courtship ideals, and marriage and family life. But in the 1990s, those benefits were still in the future; the theology of the body was a seed which needed time and the right conditions to flourish. Our family was caught between the confusion of the "Church That's Happening Now" with poor leadership in how to raise faithful Catholic young people, and the promise of a springtime of the Faith. As I write now 25 years later, there is much evidence of this springtime, with many apostolates dedicated to forming Catholics in their faith, strengthening marriages, discipling young people, and providing vibrant Catholic education. We, however, flew by the seat of our pants, so to speak. As a convert to Catholicism, I had no experience of the patrimony of wisdom of the Church. I lived in an area with a dearth of Catholic leaders who could help light our way. There were few Catholics who had successfully

---

[60] Adolfo J. Castaneda, "What is the Theology of the Body?" Human Life International, www.hli.org (accessed November 22, 2020)

gone before us and were able to mentor us. Neither side of our family was Catholic.

It seemed that Catholics typically lagged behind Protestants in helping families with practical matters, and as I had such strong Protestant roots, I tended to gravitate there for help. Dr. Raymond and Dorothy Moore, for example, in the early years of homeschooling, and Dr. James Dobson with *Focus on the Family*, who helped shape my ideas for discipline, Mary Pride and her manifesto, *The Way Home: Beyond Feminism, Back to Reality*, and even Joshua Harris' views on dating and courtship in his book, *I Kissed Dating Goodbye;* all were part of this tension in my life between non-Catholic perspectives and the Catholic truth that the few apostolates like CCL and Seton Home Study School taught through the NFP and homeschooling ministries. We were very excited to learn of the Holy Father's teaching on the theology of the body; we just didn't know how to utilize it practically in our family.

The apologetics, catechism, and theology of the body classes were invigorating our Catholic faith and it was a very educational and fulfilling time, but it was also discouraging to know there was tension with our local priests. When "funny business" began in our local parishes, with altered language in the liturgy, crucial parts of the Mass omitted, and clear departures from Catholic teaching in word and example,

9 Pray Always

several attempts were made by the laity to engage the bishop in our concerns. This only made the strained relationships worse, and frustration grew. I quote now from an editorial in the *Catholic Radio Update*, written by Michael Dorner right after Mother Angelica of EWTN had passed away on Easter Sunday 2016.

> You have no idea how bad things got in the 1970s and 1980s. We had Looney-Tunes Masses, everything from "Let's all sit around the campfire holding hands" Masses to "hootenanny Masses" to "jazz Masses" to "clown Masses" to Masses in which the priest, often dressed only in stole and alb, or even in city clothes, sat down and *ad libbed* much of the Mass. At a house-warming Mass I attended, a priest came in wearing khaki shirt and khaki pants, sat down at the dining room table, used his hosts' best china, and said Mass sitting down while the rest of us found whatever chair we could. Stories abounded in the conservative, traditionalist press about the liturgical aberrations.
>
> We had theological aberrations, too. One nun told a class, "I don't care whether there are three Persons in the Blessed Trinity or four, it doesn't matter." I heard of religious brothers and nuns telling their

9 Pray Always

classes of high school kids, "If you don't get anything out of Mass, perhaps you shouldn't go." Others assured their students that making love was moral for unmarried people "if there was genuine love and regard for the other person." No less than a nun heading the Catholic Theological Society wrote a pamphlet on just that matter with just that conclusion. Kids were told that their consciences were supreme, even over Church teaching. Across the nation, bishops one by one caved into the radicals on many issues, principally those of catechetics and liturgy.

I bring all this up because you good young [people]—young being anyone in my book under fifty—have no idea just how bad it was. It got to the point where many Catholics simply gave up and stopped going to Mass or joined the Orthodox or Protestants. One day while going down a corridor from a government office with which I had conducted business, I was stopped by a middle-aged secretary. She had heard I was big on the Faith, and she wanted to tell me that she and her husband had given up in discouragement with the Church and had joined the Presbyterian Church. "We have had enough, Mike! We have had enough!" she exclaimed from the heart. Her act was not rare. Orthodox Church priests have

9 *Pray Always*

told me in several cities that they have a number of former Catholics in each of their congregations. The big Protestant churches in New Orleans told a local reporter that as many as 40 percent of their congregation is ex-Catholic. I have read and heard stories of many older folks who, appalled by the absolute anarchy going on in the Catholic Church, simply stopped going to Mass, period. Complaints to bishops and other Catholic officials have been ignored.

Things had gotten so bad by the 1980s that I frequently prayed, "Dear Jesus, do You see what is going on in your Church? Don't You care? Well, if You don't care, then why should I? I'll simply go to Mass on Sunday and say my prayers and not concern myself with your Church anymore." Several times I was asked by concerned Orthodox and Protestants, "What is happening to the Catholic Church?"[61]

This was the state of the Church when I converted to Catholicism and as Ed and I raised our family. This was what our little group, *Why Be Catholic?* was up against. I remember telling an acquaintance about it in exasperation with the

---

[61] Michael Dorner, "Mother Angelica—A Personal Perspective," Catholic Radio Update #800, 6. Used with permission.

9 Pray Always

words, "We just want to be Catholic!" Our frustration led us to make plenty of mistakes along the way, including at times a lack of charity and harboring prideful self-righteousness.

In 1997, Ed took a sabbatical year to write an electronics textbook. Interspersed with his computer time, he wanted to finish a small 14' x 14' log cabin back in the woods that he began earlier. He started by felling red pine logs from our woods and using the tractor to haul them near the construction site. Then it became quite the family construction project of peeling and scrubbing the logs, mixing mortar, and supporting Ed, the brains behind the project. It took him over a year, but during Christmas break of 1998, my brother Randy and his family came over and helped put the finishing touches on our little cabin. While Ed's book was put to good use in his department at FSU, it never did get published and is lying in a box upstairs. The cabin still stands though.

My journal entry for October 3, 1997 reads:

Grandma Alice died today, on a beautiful warm fall day. How I loved my grandma, and how I have missed her the last two years.

Thank you God for the time I spent with her in July. I will never forget seeing her waving goodbye out the window of the nursing home as I drove away.

Oh Grandma, I love you. I'm sorry I didn't get to

9   Pray Always

be with you very much. Please forgive me. God, please take her to be with You.

Grandma is the one who accepted my husband; she is the one who received our news of another child with happiness...every time. Grandma knew what it is like for me to homeschool, and she was proud of me. Grandma has always been my dear friend.

One night sometime late in the year 2000, I couldn't sleep. I felt this urgency to write down thoughts about organizing a homeschooling conference in our local town; we still had very few Catholic homeschoolers in the area. I like to think it was with the Holy Spirit's inspiration, along with the experience of working with the Couple to Couple League's natural family planning convention in 1992, as I was able to sketch out a day-long conference with topics and speakers. I wanted to try to entice, or at least pique the interest of, local Catholics to think and pray about the possibility of homeschooling. The topics ranged from reasons for homeschooling to legal aspects to academic results. St. Patrick's Day, 2001 saw a handful of local families attending the seminar at the familiar hospital meeting room, and I was encouraged to see some families from neighboring towns too. I considered it a success, because one of these families—that I know of—did decide to join the homeschooling ranks.

9   Pray Always

In the summer of 2001, my brother, Randy, gave me a book which I dismissed as too radical and which I didn't take seriously. Oddly enough, it was a cookbook—*Nourishing Traditions* by Sally Fallon. I skimmed through it and set it aside. Some time later, I drove Heidi to a repair shop for her newly-acquired first car. The shop was quite a distance away, so we stayed close by and waited for the lengthy repairs to be made. I took this opportunity to read in detail the extensive educational material in this cookbook, which was so unlike any other I'd read. (The subtitle says it all: *The Cookbook that Challenges Politically Correct Nutrition and the Diet Dictocrats*.) I was still somewhat skeptical after this detailed read, but the author opened my mind to ideas that did resonate with me. This was another book that impacted my life and my family's life in years to come...just not yet.

Joseph graduated from Franciscan University of Steubenville in 2001. Heidi had attended there for several semesters too (though she graduated with her nursing degree from Ferris State University, where her dad taught). When we attended Joseph's graduation, he and Heidi gave me a beautiful Mother's Day gift that I will always remember. They knew one of my favorite Christian songs, "Shout to the Lord," and they played a music CD of it as they sang it together for me. I felt very blessed to have such thoughtful children.

9 Pray Always

Later that summer, the three musketeers of the *Why Be Catholic?* group, Brigid, Diane, and I, felt a call to consecrate ourselves to the Blessed Mother. We picked a date to begin the consecration prayers and then arranged to meet at Christ the King parish (the one where Ed and I had seen and talked with his sister, Sue) on Consecration Day. When that day arrived, we prayed together after Mass. I didn't feel any particular change in my life then, but as I look back now, I see that our Blessed Mother was preparing me for what I call "The Sorrowful Years."

10
Why Does the Sun go on Shining?

In 2002, the landline telephone in our house was still the messenger of joy and glad tidings or of tragedy and sorrow. One June afternoon, my mother called. She and my dad were traveling to Michigan from Texas where they had lived for the last decade. They were celebrating their 50th wedding anniversary, June 17, by returning to their home state of Michigan for an anniversary party at my Aunt Arlene's church. We were all looking forward to this joyous occasion, and Aunt Arlene was a favorite of our family. Mom told me on the phone that as they neared the town where Aunt Arlene lived, there was an accident on the road and traffic had been re-routed around it. My parents were able to see that it had been a tragedy. She went on to tell me that when they got to Aunt Arlene's home, she wasn't there but had left a note saying that she had an eye doctor appointment and would be home soon. They let themselves in and unloaded their belongings, as they were staying with her while in Michigan. Aunt Arlene never returned home. On the phone, my mother told me it was Aunt Arlene in the accident they had passed and she was killed. I shrieked, "No!" and groaned and began crying. My mother and I remained on the phone for some time, trying to make sense of it all and make some sort of plans to move forward. Afterwards, I gathered the children to break the news to them.

In my mind, this is the beginning of our sorrowful years, but they had really begun several months earlier with Ed's perplexing physical and mental symptoms. He had become very depressed and withdrawn, along with certain physical symptoms which caused him to visit the local doctor. The doctor sent him home with a prescription for an antidepressant (which I don't think he ever took) and I resigned myself to living with his depression. Soon, physical symptoms appeared. He complained of a headache periodically which affected his driving ability. This happened around the time of Aunt Arlene's death and Mom and Dad's anniversary party (which we all decided should still take place after the funeral). I remember being worried when Ed had to drive four hours home alone for a work obligation after the party.

Each July for the past several years we had hosted a homeschooling family party at our house. There were always many children running around while the parents set out food and talked. This particular year, Rachel had decided to prepare as many pastries and desserts as could fill our dining room table. It was a happy, "sweet" gathering, but two of the fathers who attended spoke to me privately about their concerns for Ed. By this time, he had begun tripping over his left foot, as if he couldn't lift it properly when walking, and the left side of his mouth didn't move with the rest of his mouth. I wondered if he just found a different way to smile, but pondered over it. He planned to travel to the Companions of Christ the Lamb retreat center in the Upper Peninsula of Michigan for a week-long private wilderness retreat in August. I insisted he return to the doctor before this trip, and I also recommended that a C-T scan of his head be done. He agreed.

Soon, the events at the beginning of this book took place. The doctor called. Tears. Prayer. Phone call to my parents who had just returned to Texas. As soon as Mom answered, she heard it in my voice and said, "What's wrong?" When I told her what the doctor had said, that Ed had a mass in his brain, she asked if I wanted them to travel back to Michigan. I told her no, not until we knew more about what was happening. She must have called my brother Randy, because he called soon and said he and his wife, Shirley, were on their way to our house. (A few days later, their oldest son, Joshua, came over and without asking or any fanfare, quietly cleaned the bathroom and the kitchen. I will always remember this kindness.)

The doctor had given us the name of a neurologist in Grand Rapids, so Monday morning I made an appointment. Randy drove us there, as neither Ed nor I was in any condition to drive. The neurologist ordered an immediate MRI, which led to the diagnosis of glioblastoma multiforme, the most lethal form of brain tumors. (Here's a plug for the American medical system, whether one agrees with the way it's run or not. When Joseph, our oldest son who had graduated from Franciscan University of Steubenville, told a fellow student and good friend from Toronto about Ed's MRI, the friend could hardly believe that he had gotten one so soon. He said in Canada it would have taken eight months. I have often remarked that Ed would have been dead long before that.) The neurologist recommended surgery right away.

I contacted our Catholic homeschooling friends for prayer and help with discernment about where to have the surgery done. We decided on a novena to St. Thérèse, the Little Flower, who has interceded for untold numbers of people and sent "spiritual roses" for reassurance that their prayers have been heard. While at the doctor's office, there happened to be an article in a news magazine that rated the top hospitals and departments in the country. Neurology at Henry Ford Hospital in Detroit came out quite near the top that year and when I called them, the neurologist's name was Rosenblum....rose in bloom! I was sure that was where Ed's surgery should take place.

And that it did, on the Feast of the Assumption, Mary's entrance into heaven, August 15. That day, when it was over and I wearily left the hospital to stay at a friend's house in

10 *Why Does the Sun Go on Shining?*

Detroit, a rainbow appeared in the sky. I thanked our Lady and our good God for this sign of their care.

While I was at our friends' home, my brother, Ken called. I remember telling him, "I feel like I am on a train taking me where I don't want to go and I can't get off." While Ed and I were in Detroit, our youngest son, Ian, stayed with our Grand Rapids friends and the older kids came to see their dad as often as they could. Our friend, Drew, drove hours to visit Ed as well. It all seemed like an unbelievable dream.

The "debulking" surgery was quite successful, as far as this type can go. These tumors are notorious for always coming back. The surgeon recommended we seek out chemotherapy and/or radiation after a time of recovery. Ed had enough medical knowledge from his years in medical school that he knew these options offered little hope of a cure. Chemo was nearly useless, and I couldn't stand the thought of radiating his brain. The radiation oncologist, who showed much compassion during our interview with her, suggested our daughter Heidi's wedding be moved up from December to September. We realized that she thought it possible Ed would not be able to participate in a December wedding. After we left the small-town clinic, we walked around the parking lot praying and talking. The leaves were beginning to turn color and it was lovely outside. When we got home Ed called his childhood friend who was now a priest, Father Morrow, to ask

10 Why Does the Sun Go on Shining?

what church teaching is on end of life care. Father Morrow assured him that he was not obligated to pursue treatment in his case. The *Catechism of the Catholic Church* states in paragraph 2278:

> Discontinuing medical procedures that are burdensome, dangerous, extraordinary, or disproportionate to the expected outcome can be legitimate; it is the refusal of "over-zealous" treatment. Here one does not will to cause death; one's inability to impede it is merely accepted. The decisions should be made by the patient if he is competent and able or, if not, by those legally entitled to act for the patient, whose reasonable will and legitimate interests must always be respected.

Ed decided to seek no further treatment. Our family enjoyed a lovely month of September, with Ed nearly his old self and Joseph home from school. When we had brought up the possibility of fast-tracking Heidi's wedding after the oncologist's suggestion, she and her fiancé, Ryan, were agreeable and worked feverishly to plan a beautiful wedding, celebrated on September 12. I, however, spent most waking moments researching alternative medicine that might help Ed. I could sleep no more than four hours a night and I didn't feel like eating so I lost weight. Stress caused arthritis in my joints to flare up. There were the children to care for: Rachel, Lincoln, and Ian were still living at home. Thankfully, I had already planned the next school year's curriculum for Lincoln and Ian so that was in place. (Rachel had just graduated.) I discovered a clinic in Texas that seemed to be having success in treating several types of cancer, particularly brain cancer. The treatment involved a substance the doctor called antineoplastins. Though this man, Dr. Burzynski, was viewed with skepticism and faced much persecution from mainstream medicine, he was now participating in a government clinical trial. The success statistics and patient testimonials convinced me to communicate with the team of doctors there in Houston to see if they could help Ed. I sent them his MRI results to examine, then started thinking of ways we might pay for this treatment. Alternative medicine is typically not covered by health insurance, so the majority of the expenses must be covered by the patient. Ed and I had purchased some precious metals years before and I thought they might suffice. Ed did not want to pursue alternative care and gave me no encouragement or help, though he was not unpleasant about it. I believe that he eventually submitted to the treatment in humility, for my sake. I feverishly began preparing for the trip to Houston. We would be there for about two weeks. Who would care for the children while we were gone? Our dear

10   *Why Does the Sun Go on Shining?*

friend, Vicki, whom we had met in the Wisconsin restaurant parking lot years earlier and who was now homeschooling her own children, offered to stay with them at our house. What a sacrificial gift from her and her family! My parents returned to Michigan and offered to drive Ed and I to Houston. So it was decided. We left for Texas in October.

Houston! I had never been there before and it was my first experience of stepping outside of an air conditioned building and not being able to breathe! I couldn't believe the heat and humidity, which took one's breath away. We stayed at a hotel that hosted many other patients from the clinic. We built friendships with several of them, including some Amish patients. Ed had to have a catheter inserted in his chest for the continuous IV drip of medication and I had to learn how to care for this site carefully, as well as plan his medication schedule, change the IV bags, monitor his vital signs, arrange travel for various tests, and cook and care for his physical needs. Having nursing experience was very helpful. My stress level was high, and Ed's must have been too, but he did not complain too much. He slept a lot. One day I looked for a private place to cry out to God. I felt like my soul would burst with anxiety and worry. The only place I could find was an empty stairwell, where I sat on a step and cried and cried and prayed for God's help. I felt better afterwards and I decided to ask Rachel to fly down to cook for us (she had become quite proficient and seemed to enjoy cooking). I knew it was a lot to ask of her, but she magnanimously agreed. What relief I felt! Not only to have her help, but her presence was a great comfort to me.

There were other consolations during our stay there, the greatest of which was that the hotel was located within walking distance of the Archdiocese of Galveston-Houston seminary. The first time Ed and I found it, we also discovered the chapel and the Blessed Sacrament! Oh, how Jesus' Presence ministered to us with His peace! We walked there as often as we could...we were both so thankful to have found Him. Also my parents drove from NE Texas down to see us, and the friendships we'd formed with the clinic patients were reassuring.

As we returned home with the continuous IV medication treatment (which could last many months), I remained hopeful. There would be frequent communication between the doctors and myself about adjusting Ed's oral medications and thrice-weekly blood test results, along with regular MRIs. It was now November and I resumed homeschooling Lincoln and Ian where dear friend Vicki had left off when she returned home. Joseph was privileged to attend the University of St. Andrews in Scotland for graduate school that year and had departed earlier. I became concerned about the approach of winter. That driveway...I could hire someone to clear it of snow, but it could drift shut so easily and so frequently and it was so long that it would cost a fortune and I'd still not be sure that I could get in or out when I needed to. Ed's IV medication was delivered by FedEx and they needed access at all times.

A generous offer came from a dear, distinguished friend, Annette Kirk of the Russell Kirk Center in Mecosta. (Russell Kirk, 1918-1994, is highly regarded as the author of *The Conservative Mind,* published in 1953, one of the most widely reviewed and discussed studies of political ideas in America; the book catapulted Kirk to national prominence.)[62] The Kirk Center hosts seminars, research, and fellowship opportunities in a unique, residential library and conference center with the goal of conveying to rising generations an understanding of the process by which a healthy culture is transmitted from age to age. These activities, rooted in one of American conservatism's historic places (Russell Kirk's ancestral home), bring together a lively educational community of students, young and old, professionals of many disciplines, and politicians.[63] Our family lived not far from the Center and had often participated in seminars and lectures there. Annette Kirk

---

[62] "About Russell Kirk," Russell Kirk Center, www.kirkcenter.org (accessed November 24, 2020).

[63] Ibid.

and the Center were major factors in Joseph's higher education, as well as a haven for us during Ed's illness.

Annette offered one of the houses that the Kirk Center utilizes for the frequent stays of students to us for the winter. How grateful I was to accept this offer! We packed up and moved on a cold November day to the Kirk Center, which would be not only a respite from the relentless snow drifts, but a comfortable yet stimulating environment for Ed. We were able to continue our homeschooling, Ed's medical treatments, and even participate in on-going events at the Center. Russell Kirk's extensive library was a favorite place of peace for Ed. And Annette became a trusted friend and confidante through the tremendous trials I was undergoing with caring for Ed and our family.

Rachel lived with Annette in the lovely main house, with its beautiful Italianate architecture and sculptures, coming over to our house to help with cooking and entertaining Ian. He was just turning seven, so his school consisted of informal learning for the time being. A talking globe was his favorite—and very effective—educational toy, as he memorized every single one of the countries in the world! Lincoln joined the U.S. Naval Sea Cadet Corps, a youth leadership development program sponsored by the U.S. Navy. He traveled to a nearby city for regular hands-on and experiential training in Navy operations, community service, and citizenship. He was a freshman in high school and managed to achieve high marks in his classes, even though I was unable to help much, especially with geometry. God always provides! We had some friends who lived an hour or so away. They had a son a bit older than Lincoln who was a whiz in math. Lincoln called him and was able to visit with him regularly, receiving the help he needed.

Another example of God's generous providence during this stressful time was the financial help that came our way. Ed taught during the school year of 2001-2002, but he was unable to return to school after his brain surgery in the summer of 2002. He had accrued quite a bit of sick time, allowing him to be paid for a while, but it eventually ran out. I was oblivious to this, because his fellow faculty members donated their own sick time to Ed so we had a continuous stream of income. No one ever told me this until several years later. I remember marveling that Ed's sick time lasted so long! Many faculty donated direct deposits from their accounts into ours regularly. An anonymous donor sent us a cashier's check for $50 every week. I never learned who this was. (If you are reading this, know how grateful I am to you!) As amazing as these miracles of generosity were, the biggest miracle came through the insurance company. I received a large invoice, over $30,000, from the Houston clinic long after we returned home. Much to my surprise, one day a statement arrived from

10 *Why Does the Sun Go on Shining?*

the insurance company informing me that this certain small amount had been paid; the next day another statement arrived with the same message, but a different payment. Periodically, statement after statement arrived paying more charges. Eventually, the entire $31,000 was paid for by the insurance company! This remains a mystery to me, but I know it's not a mystery to our compassionate Father God!

Near the end of our stay at the Kirk Center, in February 2003, Ed's care became quite involved with ever-increasing dosages of the medication. I needed more help from family and friends. I taught Lincoln how to change the medication IV bags, with Heidi's help. Heidi was a nursing student and was very busy with school, as well as being a newlywed, but she visited us when she could. Shirley, my sister-in-law, and her daughter each stayed with us for a week. Drew, the husband of my nursing school friend, Pam, spent a night with us when Ed was having seizures. The homeschooling friends from Grand Rapids visited often with much-needed encouragement, and Ed's childhood friends—including his priest friend—visited too. Many other people supported us with untold acts of service and prayer.

The threat of snowstorms gradually lessened and in March, we moved back home. Ed's latest MRI showed some tumor growth, and he decided he wanted to discontinue all treatments. This was a respite for him, and he was able to

10 Why Does the Sun Go on Shining?

resume limited physical and mental activity. We looked forward to a short visit home from Joseph before he took a trip to Rome, so we planned to celebrate Lincoln's 15th birthday and Ed's 55th birthday together at the end of the month, as they occurred only two days apart. We also tentatively planned a trip to Montreal, Quebec to St. Joseph's shrine, where many healings had occurred, to ask for Ed's healing. His sister, Sue, and her husband, Jack, were to travel with us not only to pray for Ed, but to visit that area, where their paternal grandmother was from. (They believed she was related to St. Andre Bessette, the humble porter who was devoted to St. Joseph and was the driving force behind the construction of St. Joseph's Oratory in Montreal.) We celebrated the birthdays and the next Sunday, just before we dropped off Joseph at the airport for his trip, we attended church together at a parish where a dear priest friend, Father Pettit, celebrated the Mass. In the narthex after Mass, Ed proclaimed to the family and friends gathered there, "I am thankful for 55 years of life!" They were the last words Joseph would remember ever hearing his father say.

Ed's last day of life on earth came two days later on Tuesday, April 8, 2003. He lay on the living room couch while Lincoln rubbed his feet throughout the day. He was suffering from an extremely sore throat. It was difficult for him to speak and impossible for him to eat or drink. Two times that afternoon he painstakingly told me that his throat was swelling, that he was going to die, and that he would miss me. He then took my hand and shook it. I dismissed his words in my mind, not believing him! Heidi had come over about 12:30 PM and had spent the afternoon and early evening with us, but Ed seemed detached from everyone. It had become sunny, though still cold out; Ed got up off the couch, put wood in the stove, and opened the living room slider door to breathe the fresh air. We tried several things to alleviate or diminish his throat pain, but nothing seemed to work.

As Ian was preparing for bed, he spoke softly to me, "Mom, I'm afraid that Dad is dying."

I replied, "No, he has a bad sore throat, but the tumor is stable and not growing very fast. He is okay."

Later, when tucking him into bed, we talked about Brother Andre, St. Joseph, and going to Montreal. Then Ian thoughtfully gazed up at me and said, "Mom, if the bags [the IV bags of medicine] are not working anymore, wouldn't it be better for us to pray for Dad to go?"

I was taken aback and couldn't answer. Eventually I said, "Yes, I suppose it would be." How could I say that, you may ask? Well, don't we teach our children that this life is but a preparation for our real home, for a life of love with the Holy Trinity? Don't we teach our children that heaven is a better place?

He then asked, "Why don't we pray that prayer right now?" I could not do that; I could not pray for my husband's death. I remained quiet, as did Ian. After several still moments, I lay down beside him until he drifted off to sleep.

I returned upstairs and ground some pain/sleep pills into frozen, blended peaches and brought it to Ed in the hopes that it might help his throat feel better and that he could sleep well. He took a few sips and I encouraged him to try to finish it. I went up to my bedroom to get ready for bed then wrote an email. My brother Randy called at 10:30 PM and I told him about Ed's sore throat. About 10:45 PM I returned downstairs. It was dark, and Ed seemed to be lying comfortably, taking deep, even breaths. A few moments later he was moving his hands and arms so I knew he was awake, but I didn't want to bother him so I just continued upstairs to bed.

A loud noise awakened me at 12:33 AM. I knew it was Ed; I thought he had dropped something large, and I waited to hear him pick it up. I heard nothing. I then became a bit alarmed, thinking he had fallen and gotten hurt. Then I thought maybe I had just dreamed I heard a noise. No, I knew I had to get up and see what had happened.

At 12:36 AM I got up fearfully and went downstairs. The couch where Ed had been lying was empty. I carefully walked over to where the light was on in the bathroom. There, on the floor, was my dear husband, lying flat on his back. I screamed and ran to him, calling his name and picking up his head. His face was ashen-colored, slightly blue; his eyes were nearly closed and he did not answer me. I ran to Rachel's bedroom, which was near the bathroom, and screamed at her closed door, "Rachel, I need you!" She got up and together we tried to see if Ed was breathing or had a pulse. No. Rachel asked if she should call 911. I said no, Dad didn't want that. We were crying and praying. She phoned Heidi and then went down to awaken Lincoln. He came upstairs and held Ed's back upright while Rachel talked about all the things we knew about our faith in God—Ed was meeting Jesus right now, that he didn't have to suffer from the tumor anymore, and many other things. I was so thankful for her and for Lincoln during these moments. It was all very traumatic, but they held up so well, unlike me, who couldn't stop crying. Rachel called the hospice nurse and then got Ian up. He was so sleepy that he stayed up only a few minutes, then wanted to go back to bed, which he did. Did he understand that his dad had just died? I don't know. Rachel, Lincoln, and I sat with Ed's body and cried and prayed together. We anointed him with holy water. I gazed at a picture on the wall as I sat and held Ed. It is a picture of a man arriving in God's Kingdom, hugging Jesus, with the Father and Holy Spirit looking on. It is beautiful. I took comfort in thinking Ed must have seen that picture just before he died.

Several years later I wrote about Ed's death for CCL's *Family Foundations* magazine:

> The moments surrounding the actual event of my husband's death in our home were as sacred for me as the births of my children had been. Heaven and earth touch when a soul goes to meet our Lord. Of course, the tears of joy and awe and relief at the births of our children were not the same tears and moans and screams which accompanied the death of my spouse, but the same aura of mystery, holiness, and reverence was there. All I could do was to cling to my Lord and Savior, the giver of all graces. This grace somehow allowed me to realize that if I could only open myself to our loving Father and remain faithful to Him through this suffering, I would see His hand in my life and experience His loving mercy—mercy which I desperately needed and need every moment of every day.[64]

We never learned why Ed went to meet our Lord that day. It was simply God's time for him to go. When the agony and confusion of this time had somewhat lessened, I asked Ian if

---

[64] Fae Presley, "God's Grace Heals the Heart Wounded by the Death of a Spouse," *Family Foundations*, Volume 33, Number 4, 24.

he had prayed that prayer, the prayer for Dad to go. He said yes. (Several years later, Ian did not remember this story. I told him about it and he said, "Well, I don't remember that, but it must have been the Holy Spirit in me that made me pray that way.")

In the early stages of Ed's illness I had researched glioblastoma tumors online. Reading about the probable effects of these tumors made me nauseous and fearful. God in His mercy spared Ed almost all of these problems. He was physically mobile until the day he died. He had received the Church's sacraments frequently during his illness and had received what turned out to be Viaticum a few days before his death, when a friend brought Jesus in the Eucharist to him. He faithfully wore his brown scapular, and the homeschooling families from Grand Rapids arranged Gregorian Masses to be said for his soul. (Gregorian Masses are a series of Holy Masses traditionally offered on 30 consecutive days as soon as possible after a person's death. They are offered for an individual soul. The custom of offering Gregorian Masses for a particular soul recognizes that few people are immediately ready for heaven after death, and that, through the infinite intercessory power of Christ's sacrifice, made present in Holy Mass, a soul can be continually perfected in grace and enabled to enter finally into union with the Most Holy Trinity.)⁶⁵ What a merciful God is He!

When the hospice nurse arrived, she ascertained Ed's death and dressed his body. Part of me was thankful that she did this, but part of me wanted to do it myself or with the kids' help. It would have been the last time to feel the remaining vestiges of his warmth, to touch him tenderly, to speak to him with love. I did not do this in reality, but I have done it in my imagination.

Heidi and her husband, Ryan, had arrived by the time the funeral home workers came and took him away from me, from us. Rachel, Lincoln, Heidi and Ryan and I sat in the living room then in the dark, crying and talking and sharing memories until morning. As light began to filter through the windows, I thought, "How could it be daytime? Why is there a new day?" It seemed to me that it would always be night. I remembered excerpts of a song, "The End of the World," written by Arthur Kent and Sylvia Dee.

Why does the sun go on shining?
Why does the sea rush to shore?
Don't they know it's the end of the world?
Why do the birds go on singing?

---

⁶⁵ "What are Gregorian Masses?" The Divine Mercy, www.thedivinemercy.org (accessed November 29, 2020).

Why do the stars glow above?
Don't they know it's the end of the world?
It ended when I lost your love.

I wake up in the morning and I wonder
Why everything's the same as it was.
I can't understand, no, I can't understand
How life goes on the way it does.

Why does my heart go on beating?
Why do these eyes of mine cry?
Don't they know it's the end of the world?
It ended when you said goodbye.

I made phone calls that morning to my parents and to Diane, a friend from Grand Rapids who left her home immediately to be with me. She and another friend, AnnMarie, helped me very much with planning Ed's funeral, which was held on April 12 at St. Francis Xavier parish in Grand Rapids. This was Ed's childhood parish and one of the parishes that our family had been attending for several years. His childhood friend, Father Morrow, was the main celebrant and homilist for the funeral Mass. Ed was buried in Woodlawn Cemetery in Grand Rapids, where his parents are both buried.

The day before Ed's funeral, another priest friend, Father Jack, called me. He had heard of Ed's death and wanted to tell me something. The previous September, Father Jack had come to visit. Ed was feeling fairly well then so they were able to have a deep conversation. Father said he would never forget that conversation, that only a person preparing for death could have spoken so sincerely and humbly. He remembered seeing Ed and I walking down the driveway holding hands as he left that day, and it was so beautiful he wished he'd had a picture of it. Father sharing that memory with me was a warm consolation.

But oh, the sorrow, the pain, the loss, the loneliness and emptiness! This was not part of my plan—I didn't know how to go on or what to do. Even now as I write this more than 17 years later, the tears flow and my heart weeps. Ed, don't go! I need you! Let me go with you! How can I be a role model for our sons? I am so inadequate. I can't do this. God, take me too!

He didn't. He reminded me that my children needed their mother. As weak and wounded as I was, I put my shoulder to the plow and pushed on.

Joseph had come home for the funeral, but he had to return to Rome. He was inspired to take me along, to delay, I suppose the reality of life without Ed. Arrangements for the children's care were made and on April 22, 2003, we settled into our hotel in Rome. We attended Mass at St. Peter's in the evening, ate dinner at a restaurant, and returned to the hotel. I was lonely for Ed and a bit homesick. That night, an Italian family checked into the room across the hall. It was my first exposure to Italian family life. My, how they argued, loudly and with much gusto, accompanied by the whining of their young child. Joseph and I found it to be quite comical and a respite from my melancholy!

The next day we attended Pope St. John Paul II's papal audience and then visited the Vatican Museums. My favorite sculpture was in the Room of Constantine: a crucifix stood upright on a pedestal, while a pagan statue was toppled and broken on the table in front of it. Jesus Christ, true Man and true God, is victorious over all! The next morning we took the Scavi tour, which is the ancient burial grounds under St. Peter Basilica and where St. Peter's bones are interred...directly beneath the altar of the Basilica. Our Church is literally founded on the bones of St. Peter! We then traveled out to the catacombs along the Appian Way, a lovely road built by the Romans in the 300s. The St. Calixtus catacomb was the first Christian catacomb, with 500,000 tombs and 12 miles of tunnels underground! (These are the notes I took while in Rome; I hope I wrote those facts down correctly!)

That evening we headed for Norcia, the birthplace of St. Benedict and his sister, St. Scholastica. What a trip that was!

10 Why Does the Sun Go on Shining?

It's a miracle we arrived in one piece. We began at the train station in Rome, boarding a train for Spoleto, the nearest train stop to Norcia. Two ladies told us which stop to get off at; of course, we couldn't speak Italian and they couldn't speak English. We got off the train where they told us to, assuming it was Spoleto. It was already getting late, after 8 PM, as we asked the conductor outside if this was Spoleto. He said no, it is the next stop! So we rushed back onto the train, saw a lady and asked her the best we could if Spoleto was the next stop. She said yes. OK. We got off at the real Spoleto and learned that there were no more busses to Norcia as it was too late in the day. We could take a taxi though, for about 70 euros! We had no other choice, so into the taxi we went. It was dark by now and it began to rain. The terrain there was extremely hilly. What a wild ride it was! I am glad it was dark and I could not see over the cliffs as the driver sped around curves and passed cars with abandon. Joseph and I began to pray the rosary, but at one point I couldn't take it anymore and began to cry. Joseph took my hand and continued with the rosary for the last stretch of this crazy trip. We did arrive safely, but we had to clean out our wallets of all the euros we had for the taxi driver!

I wrote about an aspect of this trip to Norcia in the article in CCL's *Family Foundations* magazine:

The Benedictine monastery in Norcia had recently re-opened its doors with young American brothers and priests. Joseph was acquainted with one of these brothers and so we visited this monastery. I felt an intense need for Confession. There with the Benedictine abbot, I shed copious tears over my sorrow at the ways I had failed in my marriage, had failed at self-giving love. I begged forgiveness. As a penance, this holy priest translated the *"Anima Christi"* prayer from Latin and wrote it down for me to pray, emphasizing that I should especially meditate on the words, "Within Your wounds, oh Lord, hide me.[66]

After a day and a half in Norcia, we headed back to Rome for two more days of sightseeing before we left for St. Andrews, Scotland. Joseph wanted to show me where he had been studying for the last year. I was able to attend some classes with him, meet some of his friends, attend Mass at his parish, and visit the places he frequented. One evening we were in his dorm room and he read entries of his journal from last September, when Ed was feeling so well, and from Joseph's short visit home in March just before Ed's death. I

---

[66] Presley, 25.

cried and we talked of Ed and were sad together, as we missed him. I knew it would be hard for me to be at home. Another evening we attended a talk at Joseph's parish by a visiting priest. The topic was the Mass as a sacrifice and how our lives, sacrificed for another, are not wasted, but sanctified. I asked the priest a question my brother, Ken, had asked (Ken had not identified as a Christian since college days). He wanted to know why Jesus needed to be sacrificed. The priest said that it is not that God is vengeful and demands blood to be spilled, but that Jesus loved us so much he voluntarily gave all He could—sacrificed His entire life—for us. The priest encouraged me to see the question from this viewpoint, that of sacrifice for another out of love. This is what we too, are called to imitate.

Our last day at St. Andrews we hiked along the Firth of Forth to Pittenweem, a small town where Russell and Annette Kirk had a home. It was a beautiful hike, topped off with fish and chips before we caught a bus back to St. Andrews. I flew home alone on May 2, to face life without Ed.

11
Mostly Cloudy or Partly Sunny?

Reminders of Ed's love popped out here and there. That fall, Joseph was home to attend school at FSU, where Ed had taught, and my parents were up visiting too. On September 21, 2003, I wrote in my journal:

Today is a beautiful Sunday. Mom and Dad are here, it's about 68 degrees and the sun is shining. I am sitting in [the neighbor's] woods on Ed's favorite rock writing this to remember what happened today.

I was in the house with Mom and Dad when Joseph came from outside and said, "Mom, come here. There's something in the woods you should see."

So Joseph, Lincoln, Ian, and I walked on the path through the woods, past Ed's rock, and down a hill to a birch tree. Joseph said, "We were playing frisbee and it hit that tree, bounced off it, and hit this birch tree. I was looking at the birch when I saw Dad's handwriting, and that he had written that he loved Mom! I thought...Mom's gotta see this!"

There on the trunk of the birch tree Ed had drawn

11 Mostly Cloudy or Partly Sunny?

a heart and written inside it with his initials: " I love Fae! 9/15/2001.

It is really a miracle that Joseph saw it there. Oh Ed, that is such a wonderful gift to me.

Thank you for your love! I can't believe you loved me. I miss you so much.

One week later, I wrote an addendum:

I have shared this gift with others, and they are so glad to hear it. It is not only a gift for me, but for all of us, to see how God cares for us so much that He sends little miracles of love to show He is with us always.

Joseph was so moved by this experience he wrote a beautiful poem about it. His reflections encompassed bits of life in our family during the time that Ed had written his profession of love on the birch tree, namely Ian with our dog, and Ryan courting Heidi.

The Birch Tree
Boughs sway, leaves rustle,
Sun and shadows flit and tussle
Amid a deep wood, all abustle

11   Mostly Cloudy or Partly Sunny?

With hardwood and lone birch anestle
That sings the song of memory,
Passing over years of light and dark
Rain awash over white bark
And pleasant winds slender branches mark.

There he darts, there he hides,
A young lad with pup abides
Into silent thought he often slides.
Perched on father's shoulders he rides,
Or sits near him on autumnal leaves
With cold granite supporting
The silent birch alone reporting
What passes between them while consorting.

The listening birch trembles above
A buxom lass quiet with love,
Humble before Cupid she shrove
Wondering of life, she questioned of
The listening birch, in the silent wood:
"What is a man? What can he see
In this young woman, called me?
Oh, how arduous love can be!"

Autumn stroll, man of quiet gait

11 Mostly Cloudy or Partly Sunny?

Implying mind and soul of high estate
A kind father, one without hate
Admired the birch, silent moments abate,
Drew a heart and the name of a woman
Impressed into the bark, so white
A chivalrous deed, while seeming so slight,
Humble man, slender birch, a reverent sight.

Branches churn, leaves sway,
Dark winds sweep the years away.
A mournful mother with nothing to say
Happened to glance where fell a sun ray
Upon a relic, a token of love
Hark! A chance revelation!
A kiss from afar, a fading inscription
On the back of a birch, benediction.

The white birch amidst a deep wood,
Under effervescence of cool green hood
Has peered beyond the beauteous rood
That conceals familial mysteries, it could
Whisper of a presence unseen
And the love of a man now gone
Who communicated on bark: "gaze to the dawn,
Love is forever, it carols a new song."

11 Mostly Cloudy or Partly Sunny?

Rachel left for her first year of college at Our Lady Seat of Wisdom Academy in Canada that fall. She had planned to attend a year earlier with one of her best friends, but she had agreed to stay home to help me care for her father and the rest of the family. Now she was free to go.

A joyous occasion near that same time was the birth of my first grandchild, Damien. I was privileged to be present with Ryan and Heidi as my daughter labored and delivered her first baby at home. The same midwife who had attended me during Ian's birth now attended Heidi!

Joseph and Lincoln were both home that winter of 2003-2004 and together, they managed to keep the long driveway open and the woodpile stacked. Lincoln, at 15, seemed so steady and solid. Ian seemed happy. Homeschooling and homemaking kept me going. Accomplishing outward tasks seemed to be the only way to survive, to move forward. Sadly, the pain of loss and loneliness blinded me from acknowledging or helping my children's loss and pain. I thought maintaining a normal routine would be best for them. Ed and I didn't speak openly about feelings and emotions. Neither Ed's suburban family of origin nor my family of hard-working farmers did. My children were likely crying inside, with little guidance on what to do with their grief, but I was either unaware of it or unable to help them.

11 Mostly Cloudy or Partly Sunny?

And so began "the best of times and the worst of times" about a year later. Our family's emotions may not have been talked about, but they surely were felt with the highest of highs and the lowest of lows. I began to hesitantly think about re-marriage; I was lonely, yes, but I also considered it for the sake of my younger sons. I felt so inadequate as a "replacement" for their father, and I didn't want to burden Joseph with this role as he pursued higher education. Resentment is too mild of a word for what some of my children must have felt as this development unfolded. Disbelief and bewilderment, even anger, likely grew inside them. I prayed very much and read the Scriptures. Hmm, St. Paul wasn't too keen on widows remarrying (I Corinthians 7: 8). But what about those with minor children still at home? I took some comfort from the fact that St. Thomas More had re-married soon after his wife died. Close friends did not understand. But one friend, Debbie, did understand. She said something very surprising to me one day on the phone. Debbie and her family had lived in our town while her husband was attending Ferris State University. Our families had become good friends and she began homeschooling while she lived there. She now lived in Montana but we kept in close contact by phone and sporadic visits. I had confided to her that, if God saw fit, I could think about marrying again.

She promptly said, "I have a man for you to marry." Obviously, I was shocked.

When I asked who it was, and she told me, "Tim," I said, "I don't think so. I'm a homeschooling mother and I don't have any experience with complicated lives like his." Debbie had shared parts of Tim's life with me the last few years, asking for prayers for him. He had converted to the Catholic faith in 2000 while going through a traumatic divorce. Debbie hosted a rosary get-together in her home weekly and Tim had been attending this prayer gathering. She also helped out with babysitting Tim's young daughter. I knew some of the details of his tumultuous life and I didn't want anything to do with it...but I did ask Debbie a few questions about him, just out of curiosity.

"What is his last name?"

"Presley."

"You mean, like Elvis?"

"Yes." (Tim actually is related to Elvis—fourth cousin, once removed. Due to Elvis's fame, his genealogy has been well researched. Tim's brother discovered their common ancestor—their great, great, great, great grandfather, Dunnan Presley.)

Debbie belonged at that time to a Catholic women's study group and they all knew about Tim's situation. In fact, one of

11 Mostly Cloudy or Partly Sunny?

the women was homeschooling Tim's daughter along with her own family. They had been praying for Tim to find a wife.

Two weeks later, Debbie called me in a rush and breathlessly said, "Fae, he's coming over in a few minutes to cut down some trees. Can I give him your email?" I was taken by surprise (again) and without thinking, agreed. Apparently, she was adamant with Tim in encouraging him to write to me, as the next day I received an email with the subject, "Hello from Montana." He wrote:

Dear Mrs. Stuart,

My friend, Debbie, recommended I contact you. I am not sure what she has in mind that I should dialogue with you about, but figure that it is something she feels strongly enough about to explicitly suggest that I write you. And if you know Debbie well, when she sets her mind to something, it is best to accommodate her.

Debbie is very special to me, as she is the one who taught me to pray the rosary. I am a convert to the Catholic Church and came into the Church because of generous people such as Debbie and Stan [Debbie's husband]. I have been a part of their rosary group for the past five years and probably will be as long as we are both in this area. They are people who

11 Mostly Cloudy or Partly Sunny?

I line up with in matters of faith and tend to be like myself: that is, my faith in Jesus Christ is central to my entire life and all else is peripheral.

I am a single parent and cooperate with another family to homeschool my daughter, Sarah [not her real name], *in their home. I started off sending her to Catholic school and was very disappointed with the two years she spent there. Next year is uncertain and so I have not yet made plans.*

Debbie has told me a little about you, that you are strong in your faith...but beyond that, I know practically nothing of you. If you would be interested in writing, I would be happy to talk.

God bless you and your family,
Timothy Presley

After many weeks of emailing frequently back and forth, I knew I was falling in love with this man. His descriptions of his life and faith, his family and his background; stories of growing up in the Shenandoah Valley of Virginia and logging in northern Minnesota; life in the Navy; his goals and dreams...all these topics and more were written about in a vivid style that brought the person of Timothy Presley to life. We discovered we shared some of the same counter-cultural beliefs, even NFP and homeschooling. His personality seemed

11 Mostly Cloudy or Partly Sunny?

quite different than Ed's had been. When Ed was very depressed at one point, he wrote me a letter wondering how I could be free from him; he said I needed a man "who would sing with me and dance with me." I assured him I needed only him. Now, years later, I met a man who might sing and dance with me, and yes, my heart was singing.

But Tim was divorced and had not approached the Church about an inquiry into his previous relationship. He had not even mentioned it to me as a possibility. All I had learned about marriage and all I had taught my children was now in the balance. My prayers to know God's will intensified. Do I ignore what I know to be true and right to follow my heart, or do I end this relationship now?

I knew I had to end it. In what was to be my last email, I explained that I had taught my older children the importance of pursuing a relationship only with someone who was in a position to marry and who could be a suitable spouse. Tim was not in a position to marry, so I had no reason to be in relationship with him. As my hand hovered over the mouse button to send the email late one evening, I heard inside me, "Wait until morning." Typically, I send and then think, "Oh maybe I shouldn't have sent that. Too late." This time, I did not send it but resolved to do it in the morning.

The next morning, while watching Mass on EWTN, a powerful feeling of peace about Tim came over me, with

11 Mostly Cloudy or Partly Sunny?

assurance that all would be OK; just wait and pray. So I waited to send the email. And I prayed. That afternoon, an email arrived from Tim which informed me that he had decided to petition the tribunal to have his previous relationship examined for validity. I was amazed at God's timing!

Since becoming Catholic in the year 2000, and lasting until 2008, Tim experienced mystical phenomenon that caused him to seek counsel from a priest. The priest recommended that Tim write these experiences down. They filled nearly 50 pages in his journal. These were years of tremendous spiritual growth for Tim as God revealed bits of His nature. The truth of the Catholic faith was written deep in his heart and soul.

In the fall of 2003, Tim was captivated by the reading in Scripture about the prophet Elijah who visited a widow who cared for him (1 Kings 17: 7-16). Tim seemed to think he was given a mission to visit a widow or widows. He was a cantor at his parish in Montana. One Sunday a man with Down's Syndrome, who sat in the front of the church allowing Tim to see him from the choir loft, rocked back and forth and said in a loud voice, "Visita!!!" Tim somehow understood this to be directed to him, and upon investigation, translated this word as, "Visit her!"

That Christmas, Tim took a long vacation to visit his family in Minnesota, Tennessee, and Virginia. In each place,

11 Mostly Cloudy or Partly Sunny?

his family took him to visit elderly widows. He was still meditating on Elijah, so thought this might be why he had been so absorbed in this story. Yet he had the distinct impression of not having fulfilled the mission of visiting a widow. By the next spring when Tim began writing to me, it crossed his mind that maybe I was the widow.

Mother's Day 2004 was our first phone conversation. While this brought much needed joy to my heart, it also brought resentment from the children, as I spent more and more time on the phone. So in this month of May, I wanted to do something for our family together and it seemed like a good time to do it. All of the children, even Heidi and Ryan with their new baby, Damien, arranged their schedules so we could travel to Alaska. Before life moved on with its busyness, I wanted them to see the places their dad had loved and share my memories with them. We were able to visit the little log cabin that Ed and I had stayed in on our honeymoon and climb a small mountain Ed often climbed. (It was a bit much for me. I was crawling on all fours and praying for help from my guardian angel!) We stayed with the same family who had opened their home to Ed and me and our young family years ago. It was a bittersweet trip; not only because of the memories of being there with Ed, but because my heart was in turmoil over this new relationship with Tim. It seemed somehow incongruous.

11 Mostly Cloudy or Partly Sunny?

When we returned home, Tim and I thought we should meet one another face to face, so plans were made for him and his daughter, Sarah, to visit our family at our home that June. Tim's older brother, Fr. Joseph, was a Catholic priest in Illinois and Tim wanted him to meet us as well. So Tim and Sarah traveled from Montana by train to Father Joseph's parish and I drove down with Ian from Michigan to meet them there for the first time. I will always remember seeing Tim get off the train. He ambled alongside the train with a kind of rolling walk, carrying luggage, with Sarah close by. His smile was every bit as attractive to me as I had hoped, and his eyes...the bluest eyes I had ever seen. We grinned at each other and exchanged a short hug. We kept our eyes glued on one another, except when courtesy suggested we pay attention to others! Sarah was slender and tall for her age (10). She was quiet and seemed a bit shy, understandably so. She and Ian (8) talked and laughed together as we settled in to the rectory and planned our short stay in Illinois.

The five of us then drove up together to my home, where they spent a week. We asked Father Joseph each day if he would celebrate Mass for us but he had some reason every day why he couldn't or didn't. Finally, on the last day, he agreed. Without any foreknowledge or planning, the reading for that Mass was the story of Elijah visiting the widow!

11   Mostly Cloudy or Partly Sunny?

During this visit, Tim and I discussed Sarah's future education. The family which had been homeschooling her was unable to continue, and Tim was not happy with the Catholic school. She was a very sweet girl and my heart went out to her. I am a homeschooling mother; could she stay with us? Tim was agreeable; I was agreeable; would Sarah be agreeable? She actually seemed happy and excited about it, which was a bit surprising to me. She didn't seem concerned about loneliness or homesickness at all. Much later when I knew more about her background, I wondered if her attitude was shaped partly by being adopted by Tim as a four-year-old and by being cared for by various people through her young life. She was familiar with being around new people. And so it was decided that Sarah would stay with our family, at least through the summer, with plans for homeschooling in the fall. If it didn't work out, she could return to Montana, as I was planning a trip there in August.

On July 2, 2004, Tim submitted his petition for a decree of nullity to the Church marriage tribunal (a Catholic church court). "While recognizing that with the exchange of marital vows God takes two persons and makes them one flesh, the Church knows that there are times when an element necessary for a valid marriage is missing. If a person claims that something was missing from a marriage to make it invalid,

11   Mostly Cloudy or Partly Sunny?

that person has the right to seek the assistance of a tribunal."[67] Questionnaires were sent to witnesses, but Sarah's mother did not participate in the process. By the end of the year, all of the witnesses had submitted their information. Some people may think "getting an annulment" is like Catholic divorce. It is not. As this incorrect belief is so widespread, and because this topic was of the utmost importance in my relationship with Tim, I will offer some lengthy discussion of Church teaching regarding declarations of nullity.

> The Catholic Church does not acknowledge divorce. In the Catholic mindset, marriage is not merely contractual, but sacramental. It is a permanent, spiritual union formed by God, and it makes no more sense to speak of a couple becoming un-married than of a person becoming un-baptized. A divorce, the purpose of which is to dissolve an existing marriage, must then be quite impossible. This is why remarriage after divorce is considered to be adulterous; though a person may have parted ways with their first spouse, they are still married in the sacramental sense, and therefore bound to be faithful to each other according

---

[67] "Declaration of Nullity and Remarriage in the Catholic Church," Archdiocese of Oklahoma City, www.archokc.org (accessed December 9, 2020).

to the prescriptions of Christian marriage....Divorce and annulment are fundamentally different things.[68]

What then is an annulment? First of all, this terminology is misleading. The precise language should be, "What is a declaration of nullity?". The term "annulment" leads one to think that a valid, Christian marriage (in which both parties are baptized) is dissolved or annulled. This the Church tribunal cannot do. A valid, Christian marriage cannot be dissolved. A declaration of nullity means that the Church declares that "a marriage thought to be valid according to Church law actually fell short of at least one of the essential elements required for a binding union;"[69] it was never a valid marriage to begin with and the partners are free to separate and to marry if desired.

What happens in marriage? According to the article "Is Remarriage after Catholic Annulment Adultery?" on the Human Life International website,

...when a couple marries in the Catholic Church, they are bound both legally and sacramentally. They sign a

---

[68] Jenna McGuire, "Is Remarriage after Catholic Annulment Adultery?" Human Life International, www.hli.org (accessed December 8, 2020). Used with permission.

[69] "Annulments (Declaration of Nullity)," For Your Marriage, www.foryourmarriage.org (accessed December 9, 2020).

marriage contract, acknowledged by civil authorities, granting them legal married status when they file for taxes, qualification as next of kin, joint ownership of property, etc. During the ceremony, they also make sacramental vows before God and their community to regard each other according to the precepts of marriage, which are indissolubility, fidelity, and fertility. This means that their union is permanent, exclusive to the two of them, and open to the possibility of bearing children.

Divorce affects only the legal stipulations of a marriage, and it is not necessarily immoral for a married couple to contract one….In this situation [a civil divorce], the legal aspect of the marriage is dissolved, but the sacramental aspect is still in effect. Therefore, the spouses are still bound to the precept of exclusivity and cannot marry again without committing adultery. When a couple applies for a [declaration of nullity,] an investigation commences into the circumstances of their relationship at the time of the wedding. The investigation looks purely at one aspect: did a valid sacramental marriage actually take place? What canon law grounds or other aspects would apply to a possible [declaration of nullity]? For instance, if a valid marriage takes place but later the couple grows apart, or one or both spouses are unfaithful, this alone is not at all grounds for a [declaration of nullity].

To prove that a marriage is invalid, the couple must provide evidence that falls into one of a few basic categories.

One or both spouses did not freely consent to the marriage.

Because it is a personal covenant with the other spouse and with God, clear and conscious consent is absolutely indispensable to the validity of a marriage. Any marriage is invalid if one or both spouses was not of sound mind at the time of the wedding, did not understand the nature of the commitment, was not fully conscious, or was compelled by some exterior force.

The couple did not intend to follow the Catholic precepts of marriage.

Grounds of this sort might include evidence that the couple procured an abortion prior to the births of other children, indicating that they were not open to the precept of fertility. An extramarital affair could also render the marriage invalid if taking place at the time of the wedding, or if one or both of the spouses did not intend the marriage to be exclusive. Also, both spouses must understand the marriage is till "death do you part." The marriage is indissoluble. Making a prenuptial agreement, for instance, admits a possibility the marriage could end and so is not permitted. No one must be held to promises that they never made, and the vow to follow these precepts must be conscious and sincere, or the marriage is not sacramentally valid.

The couple agreed to marry for reasons other than a wish to be married to each other.

Into this category fall cases in which the couple did fully consent to marry each other, and perhaps even intended to follow the precepts of marriage, but came to this decision for the wrong reasons. For example, someone may have decided to get married so that they could come into an inheritance, or to obtain legal residence in a particular country. Marriages entered into mainly for reasons other than a vocation to live together in the divine office of matrimony are not considered to have the full validity of the sacrament.

One or both spouses deceived the other previous to the marriage on an issue that would have affected their decision to get married.

For instance, if a spouse concealed infertility before the marriage and the other spouse married them believing that they could have children together, then they might submit that as evidence that they entered into the marriage on false pretenses. Catholic couples are open to life; if one party hides infertility, this may be grounds for a declaration of nullity. Other such unwelcome surprises might include a preexisting venereal disease, previous incarceration, and a great many others. One stipulation to keep in mind is that this applies only to facts that were fully established at the time of the marriage. A wife may consider herself deceived on a grave issue if she marries a man who claimed to be a brain surgeon and turns out to be a drug smuggler, but not if she marries a man who said he was going to go to medical school to become a brain surgeon but never graduates. All commitments are made in the awareness that the future is uncertain, and a covenant does not disappear if things turn out differently than one hoped.

All these grounds for invalidity concern the circumstances *at the time of the wedding*. If a couple knowingly consented to marry each other, was undeceived about the relevant facts of each other's lives, and intended to follow the precepts of marriage in order to pursue a vocation in the office of matrimony, the marriage is valid no matter what goes wrong after that.

Many Catholics married in the Church apply for [declarations of nullity] when they have given up on the possibility of repairing their [relationship]... sometimes years after separation and divorce. The [declaration of nullity] process can be rather prolonged, but is not usually as arduous as some believe it to be. Each case is investigated by a tribunal with three judges. Once the facts are established, the tribunal will either issue or deny a declaration of nullity based on their determination of the marriage's validity.

In 2015, Pope Francis helped to streamline the process by placing responsibility for processing [the] applications on the shoulders of the local bishop and creating an avenue by which the more clear-cut cases can be processed through him directly. Tribunals were also encouraged to issue decisions promptly and free of charge whenever possible. These changes do not expand acceptable grounds for [nullity]; instead, Pope Francis has made some purely logistical adjustments so that the many Catholics who have divorced and remarried outside the church will not be held back from returning to communion by a daunting bureaucracy.[70]

Tribunals were encouraged to issue decisions promptly. The Church's 1983 *Code of Canon Law* specifies that the first decision (two courts were required to make a judgement in 2005 when Tim's case was heard) should be made within a year and the second decision in six months.[71] By the summer of 2005, one year after Tim submitted his petition, we became anxious to hear any news from the tribunal. Tim began to call the diocese regularly. Finally, in early September, he talked with one of the tribunal judges who said that nothing was happening in the tribunal at this time and not to expect any activity in the foreseeable future! Tim was angry and I was devastated. Several days later, Tim called the bishop and expressed his frustration with what he'd heard about the tribunal. The bishop agreed that it was not right for the tribunal to be inactive. He assured Tim that he would see to it that his case was resolved by the end of the year. The bishop was true to his word. On November 2, 2005 Tim received a letter from the tribunal with the news that his case had been decided by the first court and the decree of nullity was

---

[70] Jenna McGuire. Used with permission.

[71] Code of Canon Law, Latin-English Edition, Canon Law Society of America (Washington, D.C.) 1983, paragraph 1453.

11 Mostly Cloudy or Partly Sunny?

granted. The second court would still need to make its decision, but this first one was the most important. Tim had begun over-the-road trucking so he could deliver loads in Michigan and visit Sarah, Ian, and me frequently. He was away in Pennsylvania on this eventful day when I sat in the post office parking lot and read the tribunal letter to him with tears of joy and thanksgiving.

The journey of getting to this point in our relationship was a long and grueling one. For example, the Christmas of 2004, my brother, Ken, invited my parents and brother Randy and me, along with our families, to his home in Colorado. My father was dying of cancer, and we realized this would be his last Christmas. So we made it a big family get-together. I thought it would be a good time for Tim to meet my extended family, and it turned out to be the only time he would ever meet my father. It was a fruitful visit in many ways, but it was very difficult for some of my children to share their family with this stranger, Tim. They were hurting from the loss of their father and thought it was not prudent for Tim and me to be growing closer without a decree of nullity. They expressed their displeasure rather forcefully to both Tim and me.

Misunderstandings and lack of communication with my children, questions from family and friends, uncertainty of the truth of Tim's earlier attempt at marriage and the emotional rollercoaster that caused, problems within the tribunal itself,

11 *Mostly Cloudy or Partly Sunny?*

and my own failures all contributed to my angst. Jesus' words in Mark 10 swirled around in my head: "What therefore God has joined together, let no man put asunder." And, "Whoever divorces his wife and marries another, commits adultery." Would I be a party to adultery if I married Tim? Friends from Montana assured me with their opinion that Tim's was not a valid marriage, but I did not know first-hand of his past. I needed to trust the Church to discern the truth of that relationship. I did know, however, if it was found that he was, indeed, still in a valid marriage, then we would have to go our separate ways. We acknowledged this, as we both desired to abide by whatever decision the Church rendered. We saw this decision as being as close to the truth as one could get about the matter. We realized it would be very painful if the truth forced us to separate.

Yes, we had gotten the cart before the horse. We should not have fallen in love before Tim had his previous relationship scrutinized by the Church. After the divorce, his best friend encouraged him to do so right away but he saw no need to do it. He had no intention of entering into a romantic relationship. One cannot always live according to plan. Some people do decide to submit their cases to the tribunal even though they are not planning to marry in the future. They find it "helps them to understand what went wrong and why. They gain insights into themselves. Others say that the process

11 Mostly Cloudy or Partly Sunny?

allowed them to tell their whole story for the first time to someone who was willing to listen. A person cannot know today if they might want to marry in the future when crucial witnesses may be deceased or their own memories may have dimmed."[72]

Why was I willing to endure this roller coaster of emotions and risk the estrangement of some of my children over this man? Through it all I prayed to know God's will. It seemed to both Tim and me that He was leading us to pursue marriage, even as we made hurtful mistakes along the way. Though my children were having a difficult time of it, I reasoned that with the passing of time their hurt over losing their father might diminish and then they might benefit from having Tim in their lives. He was a strong Catholic and shared many of our family's values and interests. He thought seriously about spiritual matters and was not interested in wasting time on superficial pursuits. This was important to me. His sanguine personality was a bonus which brought much joy to my life. I loved him very much and hoped, if he was able to marry me, that I could be a loving wife to this man who so needed a loving wife.

---

[72] "Annulments (Declarations of Nullity)", For Your Marriage, www.foryourmarriage.org (accessed December 9, 2020).

11 Mostly Cloudy or Partly Sunny?

As my father was nearing death in February of 2005, I traveled to Texas to be with my mother and father before he died. The night just before he met Jesus, I sat up with him and sang the Chaplet of Divine Mercy over and over. This is a beautiful prayer composed by our Lord Himself to help foster devotion to His Divine Mercy. He taught it to a Polish nun, Saint Maria Faustina Kowalska in 1935, in one of His many private revelations to her. Jesus conveyed to her our need to ask for His mercy, to be merciful ourselves, and to trust in Him completely. Mercy is a key part of the love that He has for us and wants us to show each other.[73] This short prayer, which takes only six to seven minutes to pray, is "one of the most powerful prayers on the face of the earth...especially for the dying."[74] St. Faustina tells us what Jesus told her:

> My daughter, encourage souls to say the Chaplet which I have given to you. It pleases Me to grant everything they ask of Me by saying the Chaplet...
>
> Write that when they say this Chaplet in the presence of the dying, I will stand between My Father

---

[73] "The Divine Mercy Chaplet," Our Catholic Prayers, www.ourcatholicprayers.com (accessed December 29, 2020).

[74] Fr. Gabriel Lickteig, "When Demons Flee Dying Souls: The Hidden Saving Power of the Divine Mercy Chaplet," ChurchPOP, www.churchpop.com (accessed December 29, 2020).

and the dying person, not as the just Judge but as the merciful Savior" (Diary of St. Faustina, 1541).

At the hour of death, I defend as My own glory every soul that will say this chaplet; or when others say it for a dying person, the indulgence is the same (Diary of St. Faustina, 811).

How great is Jesus' mercy and love! I am thankful that I was able to be with my father and to pray for him as he died.

My mother wanted a wooden casket for my father, just like the one I chose for Ed two years earlier. Tim offered to build the casket himself; he is a skilled woodworker, but he had no shop to work in at his home in Montana. He built my father's casket in his kitchen! He then arranged for it to be delivered on the back of a semi to the funeral home in Texas. My father's body was then transported in Tim's casket to Michigan, where his funeral took place. It was here that several people commented, "That is the casket I want for my funeral." This was the inspiration for our future casket-making business, Stuart & Presley, LLC.

My mom was alone now in Texas. Winter was approaching once again in Michigan. Tim and I were not able to marry yet, as the second, and final, court decision had not arrived. The driveway problem (or should I say the snow problem) was causing me much concern, and relationships

11 Mostly Cloudy or Partly Sunny?

with some of my children were continuing to be strained. Tim and I talked about it and we decided I should move to Texas with Ian and Sarah, at least for the winter. Lincoln did not want to go with us and moved in with Heidi and Ryan. Joseph was taking a break from schooling and thought it would be an adventure to take over his grandfather's organic onion farm, so he came with us. Tim quit his trucking job to join us, in anticipation of an eventual positive decision from the second court. The moving truck just barely made it out the driveway on a snowy, late-December day, heading for a new start in Texas.

12
Joy and Anguish in the Heat of Texas

Finding a place to live was my first priority. In the event we could marry, Tim and I planned to build a small house on land purchased from my mother. I had stayed with my parents whenever I traveled to visit them, and surmised that we could stay with my mother temporarily. Mom said Tim and Joseph could live with her, but the children and I needed to stay somewhere else. She didn't think she could take living with two children. I was hurt by this and felt the sting of discrimination against a mother with young children. (I had experienced that before when Ed and I returned from Alaska and were looking for an apartment. We were told that we had too many children; we had two and I was pregnant with the third.)

So I began looking. Right across the road was a rental house owned by a friend of Mom's. I talked to the friend and it seemed like it would work, but we did a little investigating into the previous tenants. Police had actually raided the house and the tenants went to jail. We suspected that it had been a methamphetamine house, and sure enough, it was. A house used for meth production is rendered nearly unlivable, as the chemicals penetrate the house's interior quite thoroughly. There was no way I was going to have the kids live there.

There were few houses close by. We found one about 12 miles away, but the logistics of that looked problematic. Driving back and forth each day while trying to homeschool the kids, cook for Joseph and Tim (I didn't want to burden my mother with that), and work on building a house seemed too much. In the end, my mother changed her mind and let us stay with her. While this was convenient and a temporary relief in the short run, it left "a queasy feeling in the pit of my stomach as I lived in an uneasy alliance with my conscience."[75] It proved to be a mistake in the long run. Some of my children were appalled that Tim and I would be living in the same house, unmarried. Though we remained unmarried only about six weeks, it was a terrible setback for my relationship with them.

January 26, 2006...St. Timothy's feast day! We received the news that the second court decision ratified the first decision. Tim's previous relationship was declared null and he was free to marry. More tears of joy and thanksgiving! We wanted to rectify the situation of living in the occasion of sin as quickly as possible. *"Occasions of sin* are external circumstances—whether of things or persons—which either

---

[75] Marc Foley, O.C.D., *St. Thérèse of Lisieux, Story of a Soul, Study Edition* (Washington, D.C.: ICS Publications, 2019), 255.

because of their special nature or because of the frailty common to humanity or peculiar to some individual, incite or entice one to sin."[76] Marriage planning took top priority, and we chose Our Lady of Lourdes feast day, two weeks later, February 11, 2006. We wanted to be married with our family and friends present, so the wedding was to take place in Michigan at Christ the King parish where our family had worshipped and where many events had taken place: our first parish when Ed and I moved back to Michigan in 1988, Lincoln's baptism, the renewed acquaintance with Ed's sister and husband, and my consecration to our Blessed Mother.

Father Joseph, Tim's brother, presided at our simple wedding. Debbie, who had introduced us, and her husband, Stan, traveled from Montana to be our witnesses. I remember right after reciting our vows to each other, I silently mouthed the words, "We are married!" to Tim. We were so happy. This time around, my vows were time-tested and sanctioned by the Catholic Church, unlike my vows with Ed. "I, Fae, take you, Tim, for my lawful husband, to have and to hold from this day forward, for better for worse, for richer for poorer, in sickness and in health, until death do us part." We received much encouragement from friends and family who attended our wedding, but the undercurrent of resentment from some of the

---

[76] "Occasions of Sin," from *Catholic Encyclopedia*, New Advent, www.newadvent.org (accessed December 16, 2020).

children was ever present. Again, the mingling of joy and sorrow.

After a wonderful reception dinner at a nearby lodge, Tim and I headed for Holy Hill, a shrine in Wisconsin. We were looking forward to several days at this sacred place, a monastery for Carmelite friars and brothers. The Discalced Carmelites are a Roman Catholic religious community of priests, brothers, nuns, and laity serving the Church through lives of prayer and ministry, in a fraternal setting. Their roots go back to twelfth-century hermits on Mount Carmel in the Holy Land. The Discalced Carmelites were established by St. Teresa of Avila in 1562 and St. John of the Cross in 1568 to renew the Order's commitment to contemplation, simplicity, and community.[77] Little did Tim and I know then on our honeymoon, that years later we would become secular, or lay, members of the Carmelite order ourselves.

What a blessed time we enjoyed at the monastery! We were able to attend Mass every day, visit Jesus in the Blessed Sacrament any time of the day or night, make the outdoor Stations of the Cross in the snow, cook together in a private kitchen, and enjoy our new married life together. Our travel back to Texas in mid-February that year was memorable. We drove in an ice storm nearly the whole way, but Tim's truck

---

[77] "Who Are We?" Discalced Carmelite Friars, Washington Province, www.discalcedcarmel.org (accessed December 21, 2020).

12   *Joy and Anguish in the Heat of Texas*

driving skills came in handy and we arrived safely home, guided by our guardian angels.

Many projects awaited us. We began the process of purchasing some land from Mom on which to build a house, so Tim's main goal was to plan and construct the first phase—a garage that could be used as temporary living space while the house was built. He also began a woodworking business—constructing wooden funeral caskets. Joseph became skilled in organic farming, learning the regulations of certification both nationally and in Texas. He learned how to plow a straight furrow, how to plant and harvest onions, how to market onions to local stores. Mom was happy with all this activity going on around her. Ian, though sad at leaving his Michigan home, had gotten to be friends with Sarah and learned about accepting other people who are different from himself. He began to realize that one doesn't always get one's own way, and he grew in selflessness and cooperation. I was cooking for everyone and homeschooling Sarah and Ian, looking for opportunities for them to make friends and participate in outside activities. Sarah was taking piano lessons and we joined a local 4-H group which met sporadically, but the main source for their friendships grew from the Catholic homeschooling group. This was a newly-founded group by two women I had met the summer before moving to Texas.

Not long after my father had died, I was visiting Mom and

attended daily Mass at the Cathedral. A woman and her daughter sat several pews in front of me and I observed how they interacted with each other. I thought, "They seem like homeschoolers." Meeting them in the parking lot after Mass was providential. They were, indeed, homeschoolers, and we shared many common interests. Cindy, her husband, Robert, and their three children became dear friends. She was in the process of organizing the homeschooling group with another woman, Monica, and the three of us met at Cindy's home to work on it together after I had moved "down south."

Life was rich and full...and hot! We northerners weren't used to the heat and humidity, but we were willing to learn how to accommodate it. (Do not touch the steering wheel of a car that's been sitting out in the sun unless the air conditioner has been on for some time!) We learned about termites and the steps necessary to protect one's home from them, how to orient a new house to take advantage of cooling breezes and protect the interior from the sun's direct rays, what garden crops to plant and which ones not to plant. We knew how to plant potatoes up north, but had to adjust our technique for Texas. (If left in the ground after maturity, fire ants eat them.) We learned to watch for black widow spiders when picking tomatoes!

Tim had completed our little garage/home and we were enjoying having our own space, yet close to Mom and to the onion field and gardens. But we discovered we had different styles of discipline for Sarah and Ian. Tim could be fierce with rough edges and I wasn't capable of smoothing them at this point. It was a problem I wasn't able to deal with, as there were so many things going on in our family; each of my own five children had unique challenges, along with Sarah's growing unrest. When she entered adolescence, she seemed to become a different person. Homeschooling wasn't going well; I couldn't trust her to do her work honestly. She became withdrawn, secretive, argumentative, and generally disagreeable. We had come to know our parish priest fairly well and were interested in helping him with marriage preparation and counseling, as Tim and I had taken a class offered by the diocese on the canon law of marriage, taught by a canon lawyer. Our priest had some interesting ideas on passing on the Faith in a family setting, and we were enthusiastic about working with him in that area as well. But our relationship with the priest gradually grew cooler, and we wondered what was going on. We discovered that Sarah was talking to the priest and telling him things that weren't true about Tim and our family. To say there was tension in our home would be an understatement.

Holy Thursday, 2007—Tim and I were close to the sanctuary, singing in the choir for the evening Mass. When it was time for the exchange of peace, our priest came over to shake our hands. Tim and I stood beside each other. The priest shook my hand, then reached out to shake Tim's hand. As his arm extended, a large drop of bright, red blood exuded from him and landed on the *Tantum Ergo*, the next piece of music we were to sing, which was open on a music stand. Tim and I looked at each other, somehow knowing there was deep meaning in this, but remained silent. The next day, on Good Friday, Tim asked the priest if he had a wound on his hand or arm, or anything that had been bleeding. He did not. We didn't have long to meditate on this unusual experience before a possible meaning revealed itself.

A knock came at our door early on the morning of Easter Monday. Tim was working at a neighbor's house so I was home alone with the children. The woman identified herself as a worker with Child Protective Services (CPS) and asked if the police had been to our home. I said no. She said that there had been allegations of abuse by Sarah. This was completely out of the blue and I knew nothing about it. The CPS worker waited in her car while I called Tim (and the Texas Home School Coalition for advice). This incident rates right up there with one of a mother's worst nightmares. Thoughts of false accusations, jail, removal of my children from me all swirled around in my head. Thankfully, over a period of several days, after extensive interviews of Sarah, Ian, Tim, and me, all allegations were dropped and expunged from the records.

12 *Joy and Anguish in the Heat of Texas*

Several days later, in the middle of the night another knock came at the door. A policeman asked if we had a daughter named Sarah and if we knew where she was. "Yes," Tim said. "She's right here in her bed."

"No," the policeman said. "She is out in my patrol car." Sarah had left our house after we were all sleeping and ran to our parish priest's rectory. The priest immediately called the police, who returned her to our home. We learned it was the priest who had called CPS after Sarah had told him she was being abused at home, so we had no spiritual assistance during this ordeal. The relationship with our priest became an adversarial one. His lawyer even wrote us a letter telling us not to contact him in any way. We received a letter from the priest himself, filled with misunderstandings and outright falsehoods that he believed about us. Was this, then, the meaning of the priest's blood which dropped in front of us on Holy Thursday? Was it an indication of the suffering we would share with Jesus, brought by the hand of our parish priest?

The emotional and physical toll from this experience may have been a factor in my subsequent miscarriage. Tim and I were open to life in our marriage, and just a few weeks earlier I discovered I was pregnant. We had only a short time to rejoice together as we acknowledged the presence of our child; on Divine Mercy Sunday, the Sunday after Easter and only six days after the initial visit from CPS, little William was lost to us. No, we don't know if our baby was a boy or a girl, but we wanted to name the child, as Ed and I had done years earlier for MaryLeah. I wonder if the two of them have gotten acquainted.

Sarah was quite uncommunicative and distant. We attempted to draw her out, to give us some explanation, but she would not. Tim and I needed time to process all that had happened without having to constantly monitor Sarah, so we asked his brother and wife if they would be willing to care for her for a short time. They had experience in sheltering troubled children so we felt confident that she would be safe, and might even have fun. They lived on a homestead in Minnesota with gardens and animals and were neighbors of a family with many foster children. They agreed, and Sarah was more than happy to leave us later that month.

It was a very confusing time, trying to maintain normal activities of earning a living, continuing to homeschool Ian in some sort of routine, along with trying to sort out how to move forward. The stress of humiliation and lack of spiritual guidance from our parish priest impacted my emotions. We were in close contact with Tim's brother and his wife as they adjusted to Sarah's presence in their family. We prayed and sought God's will, especially for what would be helpful for Sarah. We began researching what her mental or

12 Joy and Anguish in the Heat of Texas

psychological problems might be, if there was information we could use to assist her. Should we try to find a good Catholic school for her? Should she see a psychologist or counselor? Tim and I did work with a counselor for some time and she was able to give us some guidance as to what could be behind Sarah's behavior. Finances were becoming stressful, so while Sarah was away we made a trip to Montana to prepare Tim's previous home for sale and put it on the market.

We thought it best not to return to our parish. The relationship with the pastor was much too difficult. Sarah had also become infatuated with one of the diocesan seminarians assigned to our parish, and we contemplated the difficulties that could cause. She had shown us in diverse, subtle and not so subtle ways that she was capable of causing much turmoil. We thought maybe we should return to Michigan. Sarah had enjoyed living at my home and had done well there. (We had not sold it when we moved to Texas.)

We discussed it with Mom; Joseph had since gone on to further his education. She would be alone again and I felt responsible for what seemed like abandoning her. Her health was good in Texas and she did not want to move to Michigan with us or to Colorado with my brother, Ken. God provided in a miraculous way. Tim's woodworking shop was next to Mom's house. He worked there frequently and occasionally ordered parts and supplies which arrived by UPS. The UPS driver worked with wood too and was interested in Tim's projects as they got to know one another. He knew Mom as well, from delivering her packages over the years. The driver was nearing retirement as we were making plans to return to Michigan. When he learned of the situation with Mom, he said something that would affect us and Mom for the rest of her life. He said, "I will take care of your mother." We could hardly believe our ears, but with further discussion we realized he was serious. He and his wife lived far away from their own mothers and he saw this as a way of helping someone else's mother. True to his word, they have been constant companions and helpers for Mom in every situation imaginable for over 13 years. Every time I send them a thank you or some small gift of appreciation, his wife lets us know that they don't take care of Mom for pay, but they do it because they love her. They are faithful Christians who show that, as a once common song said, "They will know we are Christians by our love." It doesn't get much better than that!

    We put our little place up for sale, began packing, and said goodbye to our life in Texas.

13
Jesus, I Trust in You Even More

Arriving back home in Michigan, many things needed our attention. The house, having been vacant for some time, was in need of repairs and upkeep. Thankfully, it was summer, so Ian was on break from homeschooling, and he seemed happy to be back home. We made arrangements for Tim's brother to bring Sarah to Michigan. Tim and I prayed about how to handle this reunion with Sarah. I was certain that homeschooling would not go well for her. She did not seem to respect me or care what I thought about her work. She needed a different authority figure in order to have some success with her education. I researched the local public school and discovered that a good friend's sister was the principal there, so I called her and discussed Sarah's situation. I was uncertain what to do.

We settled back into a homesteading lifestyle along with resuming our wooden casket-making business. Tim built a woodworking shop onto the existing garage. We both enjoyed gardening, so we worked together on rejuvenating the raised garden beds that Ed had built for me years earlier. Our similar experiences of growing up on farms was a bond which brought us close as we shared laughs and understanding about

13 Jesus, I Trust in You Even More

farm life. We raised hogs one summer to sell as organic pork to friends and neighbors. We tried to provide a wholesome life for Ian and Sarah. I learned about a Catholic boys' club in a city about 45 minutes away. One of Ian's best friends lived there and joined the club too, so once a week Ian was able to enjoy sports, food, and prayer with friends.

Life became more difficult with Sarah, however. We traveled to the nearest large city to bring her to a therapist who specialized in attachment disorders. After several sessions with him, we were dismayed to hear him tell us that there is not a lot that can "heal" children with these types of disorders, with their lack of consistent care and attention as infants. The therapist did, however, hold out hope that in the future, a good marriage could lead to some psychological and emotional healing.

I used to think that if one just provided a loving, supportive family for a troubled child that the child would thrive. I wanted to provide that for Sarah. But my experience with her, and through learning more as time went on, made this belief hard to hang on to. It seems that no matter how dysfunctional a biological family life is, a child taken out of that family will long to be reunited with its mother and/or father. Sarah did not know her biological father, she only knew her mother. I believe many of her behavioral difficulties were linked to this longing to be reunited with her mother, even though her mother had neglected her when she was a young child and had explicitly rejected her.

My concern for Ian's well-being was growing too; Sarah's increasingly troubling behavior and influence had a certain effect on Ian (he was two years younger than Sarah) that was not positive. And I was at my wits' end on how to parent this child. Arguments, devious behavior, surliness, harsh discipline were all a stew of misery. Tim and I talked about options. Is there anyone in her mother's family who could be suitable and who might take her in as a step closer to her mother without endangering Sarah?

Yes, her maternal grandmother lived in the same vicinity as Sarah's mother and had cared for Sarah several years earlier. The grandmother had maintained an interest in her welfare. Would she be open to resuming this relationship with Sarah, and would Sarah be open to being with her? Could this be beneficial for Sarah? Positive answers to these questions led to Sarah moving to Minnesota with her grandmother in late summer of 2007. She was enrolled in a small, Christian private school and enjoyed voice lessons along with singing in choir. She did well in her school subjects and seemed happy. Tim and I kept in touch with Sarah and her grandmother frequently by phone.

Trouble began again a couple of months later, with Sarah running away from her grandmother's home several times.

13 Jesus, I Trust in You Even More

Tim was on the phone with the local authorities and children's shelter repeatedly. We felt helpless. We didn't understand why she kept running away. After months of trying circumstances, Sarah eventually ended up in foster care. There are things I would like to "do over" from this season of my life, but what I regret the most is not being able to help Sarah more. I did not feel capable of understanding her or giving her what she needed. My hope is that God somehow turns all of my mistakes regarding Sarah into blessings for her eventually. Tim took consolation in the fact that she was baptized, confirmed, and educated in the Catholic Faith while in his care. Though we no longer have contact with Sarah, we remain concerned for her wellbeing and pray for her always.

~

Beginning in 2008, a problem I had experienced for many years worsened. My senses of smell and taste had gradually diminished since my first child was born, and now my nose was continually producing mucus which caused coughing, hoarseness, and nasal drip. I visited a specialist who diagnosed nasal polyps—unexplained growths in the nasal cavities and sinuses—and he recommended surgery to remove them. I was happy that this would correct the problem, but after the surgery, the physician told me I would have to take nasal steroids for the rest of my life. I did not want to hear this, and I told him I wouldn't take them. He replied, "They will grow back then."

For a few blessed months, I could smell and taste perfectly! Then, sure enough, the polyps returned and grew to a size which prevented me from breathing through my nose, from singing, and even from swallowing without popping my ears. I was introduced to a Catholic specialist and I decided to see him about my problem. His diagnosis was the same as the first physician's. He discussed the steroids with me and assured me the side effects are minimal and they would keep the polyps at bay. What seems like a simple solution to this problem became for me another moment for God to work in my life. I asked myself why I was so opposed to taking these medications. Because I was afraid of the side effects? Because I refused to acknowledge medical advances? Because I wanted sole control over my life? I couldn't answer the question specifically, but I did remember another time in my life when giving up control over my body had opened the door for God to take control...and He had done a marvelous job of it! When I could no longer control or proceed on my own during my youngest son's labor and delivery at home years ago, I finally relented and gave it to God. He was so compassionate and sped the labor along at a quickened pace to give me hope. So now, I relinquished control over my body

13 Jesus, I Trust in You Even More

and reluctantly agreed to whatever it took, even the steroids, so I could breathe.

I would have to undergo a second surgery to remove the polyps first. In preparation for that surgery I had a C-T scan so the doctor could review the extent of the polyps. Surgery was scheduled for the following week. I was looking forward to attending a retreat at the diocesan retreat house the weekend before the surgery, which was Divine Mercy weekend. The following is quoted from my testimony that was published in *Love One Another* magazine several years after this retreat.

> I was grateful that the retreat was to be a silent one, because it was difficult for me to talk in my present condition. I joyfully took part in praying the rosary, going to confession, attending Mass, listening to the talks of the retreat master, and studying the encyclical *Spe Salvi* from Pope Benedict XVI. It happened that a Mass for the sick, which included the opportunity to receive the Anointing of the Sick, was also part of the schedule. Since symptoms of my illness had intensified, I thought it would be a good thing to ask for God's help through this sacrament. On Saturday, after the evening Mass for the sick, I walked down the aisle with others who also desired healing. I was anointed with oil and surrounded by the prayer of the

13 Jesus, I Trust in You Even More

retreat master—a priest of God. I felt nothing extraordinary at that moment, but I believed that God can accomplish anything. The next day, on Divine Mercy Sunday, I departed from the retreat with the others who had gone with me. I suggested praying together the Divine Mercy Chaplet at three PM, which we did.

When I got back home, I shared my experiences with my husband and son. I excitedly told them that I had gotten to know the Pope's encyclical and had learned many things from the retreat talks. I told them about the graces I received from God through the sacraments.

In the days preceding the final check-up and scheduled surgery the next week, my condition began to improve. It was so much better that I could even breathe through one of my nostrils. I talked and swallowed easily. The cough diminished. When I saw the doctor, I told him that I was feeling better, and the only reason for that might have been the sacrament of Anointing of the Sick. (He was a faithful Catholic.) I had not been on any medications and I was not taking the steroids. The doctor examined my nose and sinuses very carefully and looked at the previous reports of the C-T scan. There was silence for several

13 Jesus, I Trust in You Even More

moments, then he finally said to me that he was unable to give a medical explanation as to why my condition had improved dramatically since the last check-up. He showed me the polyps on the scan which I had undergone just a few days ago. They had disappeared. I thanked God and great joy filled my heart![78]

I remember when the symptoms were so severe. I asked God to please let me breathe! I didn't ask for the return of smell or taste, or for complete healing. But our merciful Lord cannot be outdone in generosity. He completely removed the polyps and I cancelled the scheduled surgery. It has been 11 years since that miracle of Divine Mercy, and I am still able to smell, taste, and breathe freely! I try to remember to thank God every day that I can breathe. Jesus, I trust in You!

Speaking of smelling and tasting, it was around this time that I picked up the cookbook I had received from my brother some years earlier, *Nourishing Traditions*. The book didn't stand alone; the author had also founded an organization called the Weston A. Price Foundation (WAPF). The Weston A. Price Foundation is a nonprofit, tax-exempt charity founded in 1999 to disseminate the research of nutrition

---

[78] Fae Presley, "I Believe God Can do Everything!" *Love One Another* magazine, No. 48, 34-35.

pioneer Dr. Weston Price. The Foundation is dedicated to restoring nutrient-dense foods to the human diet through education, research and activism.[79] WAPF publishes a quarterly journal, *Wise Traditions*, and they also normally sponsor an annual conference, featuring noted speakers and activists in the field of traditional nutrition. That fall the conference was in southern Michigan so Tim and I decided to attend. We came away convinced that traditional diets are indeed, much more health-promoting than the factory-produced foodstuffs so common in this modern world. Traditional diets consist of animal foods; grains, legumes, nuts, seeds; fruits and vegetables; and fats/oils, all prepared in a time-tested way to ensure nutrient availability. WAPF is the parent organization for nearly 400 local chapters in America and around the world. Tim and I started our own local chapter, inviting neighbors and friends to monthly meetings with information not only on how and why traditional foods are beneficial, but how to prepare them. One of the friends who learned of WAPF through these meetings included a note in her Christmas card to us one year about how thankful she is for WAPF.

Local parish life had improved somewhat since Ed and I were raising our children in Michigan, so Tim, Ian, and I

---

[79] "About the Foundation," Weston A. Price Foundation, www.westonaprice.org (accessed January 15, 2021.

13 Jesus, I Trust in You Even More

attended a nearby parish. Tim and I volunteered to help teach high school religious education and Ian became an altar server. We were fairly content, though it was somewhat bittersweet for me to live in the home I had shared with Ed. There were still struggles, too, in the parish, in our family, and in the community. Instances of questionable teaching at church, continued strained relationships with some of my children, and bias from local funeral directors against our casket business left us demoralized. To us, providing less-expensive though beautiful, handmade caskets for grieving families was a ministry. To others, it was competition for the "casket market" and not welcome. Lies began to surface about our business and soon outlets we had pursued with earlier success were closed to us.

Friends had recently moved to the Upper Peninsula (U.P.) of Michigan and we visited them several times. Growing up in lower Michigan, the lure of the wild Upper Peninsula was strong for many people, including myself. Thoughts of self-sufficiency, independence, and remoteness were all part of the romance of this sparsely populated part of Michigan. Many "trolls" (nickname for Michigan residents of lower Michigan) often vacation in the U.P., with many vacationers longing for the opportunity to actually call it home. Employment opportunities are few and far between however, and the weather isn't exactly desirable either, unless winter activities are favorites. According to the article, "The Snowiest Places in America," average annual snowfall near Marquette, in the north-central U.P., is 203.3 inches![80] Upper Michigan claims the distinction as the snowiest non-mountainous location east of the Rockies.[81] Temperatures often are brutally cold as well. January 1994 saw the harshest cold blast in 117 years. On the 18th, the *high* temperature near Marquette was -15 degrees! In the small town of Amasa, the low temperature plummeted to -53 degrees early on the morning of January 19th.[82] Overall, data provided by the National Weather Service reported an average temperature in January 1994 as 2.8 degrees and in February 7.7 degrees. During the winter of 1993-1994, there were 42 days below zero, and nine days with high temperatures below zero.[83] It takes a certain type of person to want to live in those conditions!

We didn't know if we were up to the challenge of living in the U.P., but long story short, we decided to go. Several things factored into the decision: that lure of the wild, the desire for

---

[80] "The Snowiest Places in America," *www.msn.com* (accessed January 13, 2021).

[81] Karl Bohnak, *So Cold A Sky—Upper Michigan Weather Stories*, (Negaunee, Michigan: Cold Sky Publishing, 2006), 147.

[82] Bohnak, *So Cold A Sky*, 143.

[83] Ibid, 146.

rural community still alive in my heart, little hope for improvement in our relationship with my children who lived nearest us, and most importantly, what seemed to be a flourishing Catholic Diocese of Marquette. I believe that is largely due to the example and prayers of the diocese's first saintly bishop, Venerable Frederic Baraga.

The title, "venerable," is given to those people who have lived heroic virtues and are considered worthy of further consideration of sainthood. There are several steps on the road to being declared a saint by the Catholic Church. (Normally, the person must have been dead for at least five years before this process begins.)

First Step: When the subject arises that a person should be considered for sainthood, a bishop is placed in charge of the initial investigation of the person's life. If it is determined that the candidate is deemed worthy of further consideration, the Vatican grants a "Nihil Obstat." This is a Latin phrase that means "nothing hinders." Henceforth, the candidate is called a "Servant of God."

Second Step: The Church official, a Postulator, who coordinates the process and serves as an advocate, must prove that the candidate lived heroic virtues. This is achieved through the collection of documents and testimonies that are presented to the Congregation for the Causes of Saints in

Rome. When a candidate is approved, he or she earns the title of "Venerable."

Third Step: To be beatified and recognized as a "Blessed," one miracle acquired through the candidate's intercession is required in addition to recognition of heroic virtue (or martyrdom in the case of a martyr).

Fourth Step: Canonization requires a second miracle after beatification, though a Pope may waive these requirements. (A miracle is not required prior to a martyr's beatification, but one is required before his/her canonization.) Once this second miracle has been received through the candidate's intercession, the Pope declares the person a "Saint."[84]

Venerable Bishop Frederic Baraga lived a remarkable life. He was the first bishop of the Diocese of Marquette (from 1853 until 1868) and was the first of many Slovenian missionaries to come to the United States to help build up the American Catholic Church.[85] Many apostolates, organizations, counties, towns, and streets are named after him, as Catholics and non-Catholics alike believed, even before his death, that he was a saint. Stories of the miraculous events which took

---

[84] "Frequently Asked Questions Regarding Four Steps to Sainthood," www.catholicdoors.com (accessed January 14, 2021).

[85] "About Bishop Frederic Baraga," Bishop Baraga Association, www.bishopbaraga.org (accessed January 14, 2021).

place around him are told in numerous books, including *Shepherd of the Wilderness* by Bernard J. Lambert; *By Cross and Anchor* by James K. Jamison; *The Life of Bishop Baraga* by P. Chrysostomus Verwyst, O.F.M.; *The Life Story of The Most Rev. Frederick Baraga, D.D.* by Joseph Gregorich, and Bishop Baraga's own diary, *The Diary of Bishop Frederic Baraga.*

We didn't know Bishop Baraga's story when we decided to move to the U.P., but our gratitude for him steadily grew after we were officially "Yoopers," (the nickname for people who live in the U.P.). Our destination was a small town in the eastern end of the peninsula, with open fields and small farms surrounding it. We bought an old farm house on 15 acres with several outbuildings. We felt right at home amongst the parishioners at the small parish, and we were thankful for the faithfulness of the priest. Tim continued to handcraft caskets and began a short career as school bus driver. We organized another local chapter of the WAPF, which was a great way to meet neighbors and make friends.

Then we caught wind (pun intended) of a proposal to construct quite a number of massive wind turbines in our area. These turbines would surround our little acreage. We started to research this phenomenon of "wind farm" construction around the country. We met with neighbors and involved ourselves politically at the local township level. The proposal

13 Jesus, I Trust in You Even More

pitted neighbor against neighbor, as some favored it and others opposed it. The animosity got intense, and the outcome politically became more and more clear. After nearly a year of uncertainty, we thought it wise to sell our home before the turbines went up and rendered it difficult to sell. A local family signed a purchase agreement with us and we felt relieved.

However, we had no idea where we were going or how we would earn a living. One of the options we entertained was moving to South Dakota. Tim thought there may be mining jobs in that area of the country. Geology is a particular interest of his. (He had moved to Montana years earlier to pursue a geological engineering degree. After completing a year and a half in this program, he gave up that goal in order to work and care full-time for Sarah after the divorce.) So I began searching for mining jobs online. Surprise, surprise, I found an announcement for a repairman position at a mine near Marquette, the largest city in the U.P. I asked Tim if he thought he would be qualified for that. He said yes, and we decided he should pursue it. (I thought this was for a single position at the mine, but I learned later that many people were being hired.)

We did have a short-term plan—a trip to Scotland to attend Joseph's graduation from the University of Edinburgh that spring of 2010. We packed up and stored most of our

13 Jesus, I Trust in You Even More

belongings, and enjoyed a great trip to Scotland. My prayer journals from this time period record my prayers for guidance from the Holy Spirit, but I am happy to report that I didn't seem to be filled with panic and wasn't overly concerned. Maybe I was catching on that God often rescues us from our foolhardiness and brings good out of the messes we make (Romans 8: 28)!

Upon our return from Scotland we drove out to South Dakota to visit Rachel's family. On the way home (exactly where *was* home?!), we learned that it looked hopeful for Tim to be hired at the mine near Marquette. We were pleased about this, and began looking for a place to live. We did not want to purchase any real estate for a bit; renting made more sense, but finding a rural place which would accommodate our cat and dog (and Ian, who loved to wander over hill and dale with said dog), was a bit problematic. We had investigated several houses that were just not suitable and we were becoming a bit despondent.

Driving around the area near Marquette one day, we came across a lovely old farm house which, while neat and tidy, appeared to be vacant. We pulled into the short driveway and I wistfully said, "Oh, a place like this would be perfect!" Not more than two or three minutes later, a car pulled over on the side of the road in front of the house. A man approached our car and I put down my window. He said, "Can I help you folks with something?"

"Do you know anything about this house?" I asked.

"Yes, I'm doing some remodeling on it."

"Do you know who the owner is? Do you think he would be open to renting it?"

"Well, he lives in Georgia. You could call him."

The man gave us the owner's name and phone number, we thanked him, and we both drove away. I called the owner right away and, as Providence would have it, he did live in Georgia but was visiting in the U.P! He was agreeable to meeting with us and, soon, to renting his house to us. It was a great place for our family to live that first year, with open fields, woods, and plenty of room for Ian to roam. This little miracle brings such joy to my heart whenever I think about it...the builder just materialized right after we pulled into the driveway, he shared the owner's contact information, and the owner just happened to be in Marquette and open to renting his house! God can arrange anything!

14
Only One Thing is Necessary

Books, books, books! The love of reading followed me all through my life's adventures; particularly with homeschooling I was able to indulge this passion. Designing much of our children's curriculum required researching various methods and books. I chose textbooks and "required" books, as well as books for enjoyment and read-out-loud books. (Even when the kids were teens we still read out loud every evening together.) So upon our move to Marquette, I was delighted to discover a gem in the local Catholic bookstore! I spent as much time as I could there, and got to know the owners. One day while browsing, the clerk mentioned that the owners were looking for some weekend help. My heart leapt! After discussing it with Tim, I contacted the owners and was hired. Beginning in 2011, my employment there lasted years and they were years of spiritual sustenance and growth. God knows the desires of our hearts. He knew one of my dreams was to own a Catholic bookstore...but He also knew He had other plans for me and that working at the store would satisfy that dream.

In the spring of 2011 Tim, Ian, and I attended Lincoln's graduation from the Navy's Officer Candidate School (OCS)

14 Only One Thing is Necessary

in Newport, Rhode Island. He was fulfilling a long-time dream to join the U.S. Navy. I was very proud of him, as OCS is physically and psychologically grueling. He was then sent to California...so we rarely saw him for the next four years.

Ian was now a sophomore in high school; as a homeschooled student and basically an only child at this point, he desired interaction with others his age. I had met a few homeschooling families at our new parish, so I asked if there was a Catholic homeschool group in the area. The answer was no. I was disappointed but undaunted. Maybe I could help to establish one. I contacted Gayle, the first Catholic homeschool mom I had met in the area and who had many years of experience. She would know people and possibly be able to pull some strings. Sure enough, she was willing and eager to work together in this endeavor. We got to know each other while meeting to discuss ideas and share our enthusiasm about the group. Our collaboration was a great match. We each brought strengths to this project that the other lacked. My experience in Texas with the new homeschool group there was helpful, and Gayle had a good relationship with a priest who was temporarily assigned to our diocese, Father Ron. This priest was very supportive of Catholic homeschooling and he assisted us in knowing what requirements the diocese would have in order to approve the group as a Private Lay Association of the Christian Faithful.

We learned that we would need at the least, a mission statement, by-laws and statutes. I contacted my friend, Cindy, from Texas, to ask if we could model these documents after theirs. She was agreeable, so this act of generosity saved Gayle and me much time and labor.

Venerable Bishop Baraga was chosen as the group's patron saint and it was named after him: Bishop Baraga Home Educators (BBHE). With much joy, Gayle and I received the news that on March 12, 2012 Bishop Alexander Sample approved BBHE as a Private Lay Association of the Christian Faithful in the Diocese of Marquette. We held the first meeting of prospective members on May 24 of that year and sponsored our first conference in August with Fr. Ron as keynote speaker. Rounding out the program were homeschooling parents and students contributing their expertise. (Gayle and I organized the next year's conference too, but then turned over the reigns of BBHE to others.)

Things were still rather bleak for Ian though, regarding friendships with others his age. We considered other options for his education. Circumstances were different now with just one child at home and living in an area with few homeschooled high school students. We found a Catholic boarding school in Wisconsin that seemed faithful and enjoyed a good reputation. We traveled there to investigate, discussed it thoroughly with Ian, prayed, and then left the decision to him. Even though one of his good friends (from our time living in the eastern end of the U.P.) planned to attend this boarding school, Ian decided not to go.

After one year of renting our "miracle" house, we wanted to stay in the area—our parish and pastor were wonderful, Tim's job was going well, and friendships were being formed—so we began looking for real estate. We still had some desire to build our own little homestead so we purchased property that actually had some open land along with the ubiquitous woods. We spent quite a bit of time on the property, thinking and planning. I still had my house plans that I'd designed over 20 years earlier and we decided where it would be built. Then God came to our rescue again. That still, small voice in our minds got louder and louder and Tim and I both realized that this major project was probably more than we wanted to take on at our ages. We began searching for homes (already built!) that might satisfy our desire for the homesteading life.

When we found it, Tim called it the "Woodchopper's Cottage." It was a log cabin originally built in the 1950s as a hunting camp. (Here in the U.P., "camp" is the descriptive word for the place where hunters gather during hunting season. In lower Michigan, the word is "cabin." In Minnesota where Tim's family lives, it's called "shack." I find that interesting.) It had been remodeled to the extent that it could be lived in year-around. We both liked it very much so in 2011 we moved there. The location was unfamiliar to us and we didn't realize the difference location means in this part of the U.P. A change in location of even a few miles can mean the difference between a lot of snow and an unreasonably huge amount of snow! Little did we know, we had moved to the Snow Belt! Blissfully ignorant, we began working on making the place our own. Though surrounded by woods, there was an ample clearing around the house for gardens and plenty of land to roam. Tim was eager to tap the maple trees for syrup, and we considered any animals we might want on our little homestead. The house didn't have enough bedrooms for all of us, so Tim and Ian fitted a garden shed next to the house with insulation, electricity, pine paneling, and the cutest little coal/wood stove. This was Ian's "Stuey Cave." I hope he liked it; I thought it was great that he could have his own place, yet be close.

Another project I took on during this time was cleaning out and organizing our parish library. It is a beautiful little room and I saw its potential. The shelves were full to the ceiling and the floor was cluttered with many boxes of donated books and materials. I asked our pastor about someone cleaning and organizing it. He listened to me but didn't answer for quite some time. Eventually, he gave me permission to do the job. It was a labor of love which took months to accomplish. Sorting through and deciding which books to keep and which to discard was of great importance in order to keep all materials faithful to Church teaching. Everything was then organized according to subject or topic and placed on the labeled shelves. As Bishop Baraga Home Educators was active at the time, I dedicated a section of the library for lending out homeschooling materials.

After trying to inform our parishioners of the fact that the library was now open for lending books, I saw the difficulty in the library's location—it was quite inconvenient, which resulted in few parishioners taking the trouble to visit it or even to find it. While traveling in Minnesota not long afterwards, the answer to this dilemma appeared. Tim and I were entering an unfamiliar parish for Mass; close by the front entrance was a hutch filled with books! It was a lending library right where parishioners could easily access it. Excitedly I told Tim, "This is exactly what we need!" Back home, I found a suitable hutch for sale and Tim set it up in a conspicuous place at our parish. It worked so well that there are now hundreds of items checked out at any one time.

The hutch was another simple way God planted the seed of grace in my soul. "If we do not place any obstacles in its way, if we allow [the seed] to grow, it will not fail to bear fruit. It does not depend on the person who does the sowing or the reaping: God gives the growth."[86] Pope St. John Paul II said, "Every Christian has to share in the task of Christian formation. He has to feel the urgency of evangelizing...."[87] I have tried to be open to that feeling of urgency, to participate in a small way with God's saving plan. "For the love of Christ impels us...so that those who live might no longer live for themselves but for him who for their sake died and was raised" (2 Corinthians 5:14-15). I have found that engaging friends or strangers can be less challenging than connecting with certain family members. Whether we are able to verbalize the Gospel message to others or not, our lives can be the witness that may be more effective in the long run. Though I have given poor example many times, and I am prideful, selfish, and critical, I pray that, with God's grace, any efforts I have made to live an effective witness may one day bring fruit for the Master. For I know what it is to live in darkness and confusion, in sin and rebellion. As Hilaire Belloc said, "Outside the Church, it is night."

God was preparing the biggest evangelization challenge of my life, and of Tim's life, about this time. It began as Ian

---

[86] Francis Fernandez, *In Conversation with God, Vol. Three,* (New York: Scepter, 1994), 145.

[87] John Paul II, *Address*, Granada, November 15, 1982, as seen in Francis Fernandez, *In Conversation with God, Vol. Three,* (New York: Scepter Press, 1994), 83.

graduated from high school and was looking forward to a college career at the University of Mary in Bismarck, North Dakota. A faithful Catholic college, I hoped his experiences there would help him to know his vocation and to continue growing in faith. I believed he would be in good hands...his oldest brother, Joseph, was teaching there! It was by visiting Joseph that Ian became familiar with the college and decided to attend the University of Mary. So my 28 years of homeschooling had come to an end. I felt fulfilled and grateful for the opportunity to live those years together with my children. Now I felt a bit at loose ends and I prayed, "What do you want from me now, Lord?"

His answer came soon after. One evening in that summer of 2013 before Ian left for college, Tim, Ian, and I were praying the rosary with Mother Angelica and the nuns on EWTN. During the station break, an announcement came on saying that the FCC (Federal Communications Commission) was opening a window of time to receive applications for low-power FM radio licenses in October. The announcement went on to give contact information for those who might be interested in starting a Catholic radio station. Tim leaped up off the couch and said, "Did you get that phone number?!"

I said, "No, but I will." I hurriedly wrote the number down. After the rosary, Tim and I discussed the exciting possibility of bringing Catholic radio to our local area. He and

I shared a passion for Catholic radio. When he lived in Montana, one of his good friends, Greg, had started a station there so Tim was somewhat acquainted with the idea. When Ed and I were raising our young children, I listened to Christian radio during the day at times, but I often sighed and wondered why there wasn't *Catholic* radio. Ed and I dreamed of starting Catholic radio somewhere, some day. We'd even imagined what we'd name the station! That never came to pass, as Ed died before the opportunity arose. Now Tim and I wondered if this was the time and place that God might work through us to proclaim His good news on the airwaves. If this was God's will, then we wanted it too.

The low-power FM license that was mentioned in the announcement is an educational license and relatively inexpensive compared to commercial stations. As the signal is low-power it doesn't travel long distances, with a radius of only five to six miles, so it does not interfere with other broadcasters in the area. Typical holders of low-power FM licenses are schools, nonprofit organizations, and churches. One does not purchase a low-power license; it is issued by the FCC to qualified applicants during certain "windows of opportunity." These windows are few and far between as there are only a finite number of frequencies that may "fit" into the coverage map of a region without creating interference. This particular window was only the second one ever opened by the FCC; the previous one had been 13 years earlier, in 2000.

The contact number in the announcement was for the Catholic Radio Association (CRA). Before calling them, I thought about what this step might mean. Tim's work hours at the mine could be long and grueling; I would probably be the one responsible for much of this effort for the time being. (Later, Tim's knowledge and experience with electricity, electronics, and construction were crucial to this effort. It was definitely a team project—he understood the big picture and I worked on the details.) I hesitated for a moment, then took the plunge. The CRA was very helpful and outlined the steps necessary to prepare for applying for a license. One of the first requirements was that a nonprofit organization actually submit the application, so we needed to either form one ourselves or ask an existing one to take the radio project under their auspices.

A new apostolate had begun in our parish called Claves Regni Ministries (Latin for "Keys of the Kingdom") dedicated to apologetics (the defense and explanation of the teachings, beliefs, and practices of the Catholic Church). I heard that they had recently been granted nonprofit status...it seemed like this might be a good fit. I called the president of the group and explained the opportunity for a potential Catholic radio station to him. He was taken a bit by surprise, so he didn't give me an answer but invited me to present the information at their next meeting.

This would be a make or break meeting, so I prepared diligently all the information we had received from the CRA which the members would need to make a decision. I included an overview of the process of building a radio station, financial needs, equipment and personnel needs, and other concerns. I thought maybe the group itself would want to run the project, so I offered to turn it all over to them. Our pastor, Msgr. Michael, was chairman. After listening intently to all the information, he suggested that everyone spend a few moments in silent prayer seeking God's guidance. I will always remember what he said after this time of prayer: "Let's put out into the deep."

It was a dramatic moment for me. With Msgr.'s discernment in prayer, it seemed the Lord was encouraging us to take the next step. If God was not behind this project, we did not want to go forward with it. "Unless the Lord build the house, they labor in vain who build" (Psalm 127:1). The deadline for the applications to be submitted to the FCC was in the fall, merely three months away. Things were intense at the last minute getting our application in to the FCC, but just under the five PM deadline on the last day, it was successfully submitted. We received the formal construction permit in June 2014 but it was understood that construction would be underway before then. The list of things to do was long and daunting: finding a radio engineer, hiring an FCC attorney, raising money, learning how a radio station works, locating a suitable tower for the antenna, finding a studio, and numerous other concerns. God led us each step along the way. The owner of the tower which would give us the most coverage area met with us and we were able to come to an agreement (after much negotiation) to lease space for an antenna on his tower. He also referred us to his radio engineer, Coral, who was one of the biggest blessings of this project. We made arrangements to meet with him. He brought along his friend, Al, who he thought would be interested in learning about our proposal. We met at a country restaurant and got to know each other. It still seems unreal to me; these men were experts in radio broadcasting, with hectic schedules and deadlines to meet, and yet they were willing to meet with us, novices who knew nothing about radio and for all they knew, would give up and quit when the going got rough. They must have sensed our determination; by the end of our meeting they were both on board and seemed rather excited to be building a new radio station! They were both Christians, and Al was a Catholic. How providential was that!

Fundraising was of paramount importance. It all fell into place in God's timing. This is one of my favorite quotes; it is by Peter Maurin as he addressed Dorothy Day's dubiousness about starting The Catholic Worker apostolate: "In the Catholic Church, funds are never necessary. You only need to start." The initial appeal to certain select parishioners was answered generously. We applied for and received a Catholic Extension matching grant, and the Diocese of Marquette gave us a Legacy of Faith grant. (Our bishop was very supportive of the radio project.) These funds were adequate to get things off the ground; we would approach the area parishes for further pledges later in the process.

Tim and I had a crash course in all things radio; Coral and Al taught us many things, along with the Catholic Radio Association and EWTN. We decided to become EWTN affiliates, so they were of great assistance in how to run successful pledge drives in the local parishes. The parishioners came through with generosity which encouraged us greatly!

How exciting it was on the cold, snowy evening of December 16, 2014 when the engineers flipped the switch at the transmitter and told us to go out to our car and turn on the radio! There was EWTN on the new radio station, Northern Apostle Radio! It was named after, you guessed it, Venerable Bishop Baraga, whose episcopal motto was, "Only one thing is necessary." He was an apostle to the Native Americans and immigrants in the north country...the Northern Apostle.

14 Only One Thing is Necessary

Tim and I served as station managers for nearly five years, then transitioned to general managers when a talented volunteer, Kim, took over the studio duties. Northern Apostle Radio continues to proclaim the Gospel to the Marquette area, as well as throughout the U.P. and beyond through on-line streaming. "So shall my word be that goes forth from my mouth; it shall not return to me void, but shall do my will, achieving the end for which I sent it" (Isaiah 55:11). We are thankful to so many who helped in this endeavor: Coral and Al, CRA, EWTN, Claves Regni board members, Msgr. Michael, new volunteers, and importantly, generous donors and those who pray for the success of Northern Apostle Radio.

15
A Carmelite Path to the Pearl of Great Price

The relentless snowfall chased us out of our cute little log house. With Tim's hectic schedule and long hours at the mine, "taking care of it" was a burden he just didn't want to continue. We found another cute little house with outbuildings and some land south of town, in an area that receives much less snow. Here we have settled...here we have lived the longest time since we married (six years and counting).

In 2015, we learned that some fellow parishioners were inviting inquiries into the Secular Carmelites. (Secular meaning, in general, lay members of the order.) This is the same religious order which founded and whose friars live at Holy Hill in Wisconsin, where Tim and I spent our honeymoon.

The reform of the ancient Carmelite order was undertaken by St. Teresa of Avila and St. John of the Cross beginning in 1562. St. Teresa had long been a favorite saint of mine, reaching back to the days when Debbie (who had introduced Tim and me) and I lived in the same area. We studied St. Teresa, whose passion for holiness was encapsulated for me by her insistence on shunning mediocrity. Debbie and I used to remind each other not to settle for mediocrity.

15 A Carmelite Path to the Pearl of Great Price

The opportunity to learn and to be directed in prayer and contemplation by St. Teresa's religious order was exciting. Aided by their patroness, the Blessed Virgin Mary, the Carmelites have a stellar track record of having saints in their midst. St. Teresa and St. John are not the only ones. The Carmelite St. Thérèse has been called "The Greatest Saint of Modern Times!"

Tim was also attracted to the Carmelites. He had just converted to the Catholic faith in Montana when an older, "cradle Catholic" friend, a fully-professed Secular Carmelite, explained how entering into Carmelite spirituality could help him to learn about and grow in prayer. Tim began the process of formation as a Carmelite while in Montana. Then he met me, and left there. Formation was put on hold for five years. After we married and moved to the U.P., he resumed and I began the process with a small group of Carmelites at our first parish. But that was the town that was determined to erect wind turbines, the town we left. Formation was put on hold for another five years. Finally, the Carmel of the Holy Spirit in Marquette was born and Tim and I began the process all over again to be formed under the guidance of the great Carmelite saints. It takes six years of formation before one may make a final promise to live the vocation of a Secular Carmelite. It is a time of study, prayer, community, and spiritual growth. The process begins with three introductory meetings. (Our local

Carmel's Council has arranged the process a little differently than others.) If all three parties to the decision agree (the Holy Spirit, the inquiring person, and the local Carmel's Council), the person may move forward and become an aspirant. The aspirancy lasts for one year, after which the person is clothed in a large, ceremonial brown scapular.

What is a brown scapular? A scapular is an outer sleeveless garment that is part of the Carmelite "habit," or clothing. It covers the body from shoulders nearly to the feet on both front and back. So do Secular Carmelites wear this article of clothing? No, there are actually two other versions of this scapular that indicate a relationship with the Carmelite friars and/or nuns: the *ceremonial* and the *daily* scapulars. They are much smaller. Two rectangular pieces of brown cloth (as the color of the Carmelite habit is brown) are attached by two straps or strings and worn over the shoulders, with one piece worn over the chest and the other over the back. The *ceremonial* scapular cloth pieces measure about eight inches by eight inches and they are worn on the outside of the person's clothing and normally only at Carmelite functions. The small *daily* scapular measures about an inch by an inch and is worn under all clothing as a private devotion to our Blessed Mother. "It is also a sign of belonging...to the family of Carmel."⁸⁸ "The wearing of the brown scapular would be meaningless, [however,] without the wearers living and dying in the state of grace, observing chastity according to their state in life, and living a life of prayer and penitence."⁸⁹

After receiving the ceremonial scapular, the aspirant is considered a candidate and moves on to two years of formation in order to make a temporary promise. After this temporary promise, the person is considered a member of Carmel and prepares for the final, or definitive promise. This preparation lasts for three years.

"The goal of formation...goes beyond informational learning to gradual personal transformation that leads to evangelical service."⁹⁰ Gradually, oh so gradually does this take place, not only before a final promise is made but even afterwards. The goal is to know God so He may be made known. The writings of Saints Teresa of Jesus, John of the Cross, and Thérèse of the Child Jesus are sure guides to this knowledge.

Another invaluable aspect to Carmelite life is the community which fosters fraternity and bonding between

---

⁸⁸ "Scapular Catechesis," Meditations From Carmel, www.meditationsfromcarmel.com (accessed January 28, 2021).

⁸⁹ Ibid.

⁹⁰ Washington Province of the Immaculate Heart of Mary, *Book of Documents* (Washington DC:: n.p., 2017), 277.

15 A Carmelite Path to the Pearl of Great Price

fellow travelers on this formation journey. Conversation ranges from catching up on personal lives to deep spiritual insights. Concern for one another manifests in outward acts of charity for those who are ill or in need of any kind. Great reliance on prayer leads to prayer requests being shared openly with the whole community. Support in spiritual growth is frequently mentioned as one of the greatest benefits to belonging to Carmel.

There is recreation and fun too! In the past, our meetings have included presenting plays, listening to the dramatic story of the Carmelite nuns of Compiègne martyred during the French Revolution, and enjoying travelogues to Mt. Carmel in the Holy Land and to the Basilica of Our Lady of Guadalupe in Mexico.

Our local Carmel of the Holy Spirit has its roots in Mexico; this heritage is filled with heroism, miracles, and prudence. Our Carmel grew from the Monastery of the Holy Cross in Iron Mountain, Michigan. This monastery was the fruit of the Monastery of Our Lady of Guadalupe in Grand Rapids, Michigan. And that monastery's beginnings stemmed from the Carmel of Queretaro, founded in Mexico in 1803.

Because of my familiarity with the Monastery of Our Lady of Guadalupe near Grand Rapids (Ed and I and the children attended Mass there occasionally, and after Ed died I strongly considered moving near the monastery), I offered to

15 A Carmelite Path to the Pearl of Great Price

present the following story to our Carmel of the Holy Spirit. The information was obtained from a small book the Monastery published, *Carmel of Ada (Grand Rapids): Centenary Year 1916-2016*.

One of the foundresses of the Carmel of Queretaro in Mexico, Mother Elias, was born Elena Thierry and was the third youngest of 17 children. (Some sources say the second youngest of 20 children.) She was well educated, largely at home. Her mother died when she was 12 and she assumed many responsibilities that led to great maturity and preparation for the trials ahead of her. Upon discerning a religious vocation, Elena traveled by train to join a teaching order. A young religious sister approached her on the train and told Elena that she would be with that teaching order for only a short time; she would then become a Carmelite. Elena thought this very strange, of course. Sure enough, she was released from the teaching order after only a couple of years. Elena then sought to enter the Carmel in Mexico City. Arriving at the monastery, she saw a picture hanging on the wall of a young sister. It was the same sister who had approached her on the train a few years earlier! The Carmelites told her it was a picture of a sister in France, Sr. Thérèse of the Child Jesus. The day Elena saw Sr. Thérèse on the train was the exact same day she died in France, September 30, 1897!

Wave after wave of persecution of the Catholic faith began in Mexico about 1861. (This story takes place from 1910-1914.) Priests lived in 40 monasteries around Mexico and they lost them all. Foreign priests were exiled and Mexican priests were imprisoned. Nuns were carried off to prison or to the soldiers in the hills. Families were shot if found praying the rosary.

By 1913, Elena, (Sister Mary Elias) was prioress of the Carmel of Queretaro. Mother Elias's foresight, prudence, and response to Divine inspirations allowed her to disguise the sisters and live among the people, always looking for a place to live together again in community, moving from place to place and even to other cities, always in danger of death.

Eventually the Governor commanded their community to leave the country, so the first group of sisters left for Cuba—the youngest ones first, as they were most in danger from the soldiers—along with Mother Elias. They arrived in Cuba after many delays and difficulties on November 1, 1914.

Mother returned to Mexico at the end of November to bring the rest of the sisters out of the country. In Mexico City, Mother Elias and a companion, Sr. Mary of the Angels, were thrown into prison. Mother said to this Sr. Thérèse, (the French sister who had appeared to her years ago on the train) "If you really are a saint, help us out of these difficulties and don't allow us to be executed. If you do this, I will extend the

15 A Carmelite Path to the Pearl of Great Price

Carmelite order wherever I can." After days of standing on damp, dirty, stony ground in a cell with many others, Mother and Sr. Mary were ordered to be executed. They knelt down in the yard. The guards were about to blindfold them but Mother asked for it to be left off. Mother and Sr. Mary saw the guns aimed at them, heard them fire and fell on the ground. They were left for dead.

Before daylight, Mother and Sr. Mary regained consciousness and realized they were alive. They managed to escape with the help of a guard—Mother Elias warned him he would be punished if he killed them—and stumbled upon a disguised priest. He helped them get to the Shrine of Our Lady of Guadalupe in thanksgiving. That night in a hotel they examined themselves. Blood was on their habits, but there were no wounds! Mother was convinced that Sr. Thérèse was indeed a saint and had saved their lives.

They gathered up the rest of the sisters and made it to Cuba on January 8, 1915. The bishop of Grand Rapids, Michigan, Henry J. Richter, welcomed them to his diocese and they arrived there on November 2, 1915. Thus was born the Monastery of Our Lady of Guadalupe in Grand Rapids, which founded Holy Cross Monastery in Iron Mountain, which was the vine from which our secular Carmel of the Holy Spirit grew.

15 A Carmelite Path to the Pearl of Great Price

Let's return to some basics of the Secular Carmelite vocation. The Carmelite promises to strive for "evangelical perfection in the spirit of the evangelical counsels of chastity, poverty and obedience and of the Beatitudes." This promise is a pledge to pursue personal holiness,[91] and it is made under the inspiration of the Holy Spirit. Evangelical perfection means "to imitate Jesus in His love for our heavenly Father and for our fellow human beings." The Beatitudes, along with chastity (according to one's state in life), poverty and obedience, sum up our Lord's teachings. To be blessed in the Kingdom of God, one must be the servant of all.[92]

Other basic elements of this vocation are:
- To live in allegiance to Jesus Christ,[93] supported by the imitation and patronage of the most Blessed Virgin Mary;
- To seek a mysterious union with God; by way of contemplation and apostolic activity, indissolubly joined together for service to the Church;

---

[91] Washington Province, *Book of Documents* (Washington D.C.: n.p., 2017), 21.

[92] Father Hilary Doran, OCD, "Counsels and Beatitudes in Relation to the Promise," 1-2.

[93] Washington Province, "The Carmelite Rule," *Book of Documents*; 10, #2.

- To give particular importance to prayer which...is conducive to relating with God as a friend...being nourished by faith, hope, and charity;
- To infuse prayer and life with apostolic zeal;
- To live Godly self-denial and service;
- To give importance to the commitment to evangelization.[94]

It is obvious why formation is a continual process, both before and after making one's definitive promise! Tim and I have found our journey with the Carmelites to be fruitful and rewarding as we continue to ask God to guide us in His will for our lives. With His grace, and now the help of the Secular Carmelites, after years of searching and praying and learning, I hope in the end to take possession of the pearl of great price.

"Again, the kingdom of heaven is like to a merchant seeking good pearls. Who, when he had found one pearl of great price, went and sold all that he had, and bought it."

~Matthew 13:45-46

---

[94] Washington Province, *Book of Documents*, 20-21.

Epilogue

The pearl of great price has meant different things to me in different stages of my life. As a young person bereft of strong faith, it meant the sure knowledge of God's existence and love. Upon my conversion from Protestantism, the pearl of great price meant God's one, holy, catholic, and apostolic Church. This pearl is so precious to me! What jewels life-long Catholics have inherited! Though my conversion separated me from my heritage, from all that was familiar to me, and placed me in a strange and mystical world of liturgy, sacraments, traditions, and church authority, I rejoice! Growing in my faith as a wife and mother and part of the Church Militant on earth, I relentlessly sought this precious pearl of the truths and riches of Catholicism. And now, I look forward in hope as I seek the pearl of great price which is the Church in heaven, the Church Triumphant.

On September 11, 2018 I was diagnosed with a rare, aggressive form of multiple myeloma. This is a blood cancer. Plasma cells in the bone marrow run rampant, with many damaging effects. I have undergone chemotherapy, a stem cell transplant, and various alternative treatments, but the disease remains.

Epilogue

Along with managing the treatments, completing this book project has been an important goal. I am thankful that our good God gave me the time to do so.

Our local Carmel of the Holy Spirit allowed me to make my final, or definitive, promise as a Secular Carmelite a year early so that whenever my death occurs, I will have the privilege of dying as a definitively professed Carmelite.

I am eternally grateful to the people and priests, especially Msgr. Michael, who have assisted Tim and me in this trial. Numerous friends, fellow parishioners and Carmelites organized help with everything from bringing meals and housecleaning to loading our wood cookstove every day and bringing me to Mass and to chemo appointments. I cannot express how much these generous acts of love have meant to Tim and me. We are so blessed to live amongst these saintly people.

I think about the unknown journey through this cancer and how it may eventually cause my death. I think about the pain, loss of mobility, and separation from all whom I love here. Though many people pray for my healing, and I know from personal experience God performs healing miracles, it just may be that this is the way I will be born into eternal life. I trust in our Blessed Mother to intercede for me and I trust our loving Father will send His grace and consolation and extend His mercy to me when the time comes.

Epilogue

Each of us will die one day! Each of us will experience suffering in our lives and many of us will experience great suffering preceding death. This suffering can make one bitter and resentful, or it can bring about great good. What good could there possibly be? Without suffering, how would the human person learn empathy, compassion, courage, self-sacrifice, or humility? But suffering has an even greater meaning: "Christ has also raised human suffering to the level of the Redemption."[95] Christ's redemption of us sinners means that His Passion, Death, and Resurrection rescued us from the slavery of sin which came about through original sin. Our own suffering, as Pope St. John Paul II said, can serve to redeem the world if we offer our sufferings to God, united with Jesus' sacrifice.

St. Teresa Benedicta of the Cross (Edith Stein) explains this further in a letter she wrote in 1932 to a friend. St. Teresa was a Jewish convert to Catholicism who became a Carmelite nun during the WWII years. She was sent to Auschwitz by the Nazis and perished there. St. Teresa wrote:

> There is a vocation to suffer with Christ and thereby

---

[95] John Paul II, *Salvifici Doloris*, encyclical letter, Vatican website, February 11, 1984, http://www.vatican.va/content/john-paul-ii/en/apost_letters/1984/documents/hf_jp-ii_apl_11021984_salvifici-doloris.html, sec.19.

Epilogue

> to cooperate with Him in His work of salvation…And the suffering borne in union with the Lord…is His suffering, incorporated in the great work of salvation and fruitful therein. That is a fundamental premise of all…Carmelite life,…through voluntary and joyous suffering, to cooperate in the salvation of humankind.[96]

Thus, a "fundamental premise" of my Carmelite vocation has brought to fruition, through the offering of my suffering to God, the mission of evangelization and redemption of souls God has called me to.

A meditation from *Magnificat* magazine, written over 200 years ago by Father Jean-Nicolas Grou, S. J., expounds on Romans 8:28 which reads, "We know that all things work for good for those who love God, who are called according to His purpose." These are Father Grou's words:

> Saint Paul says that *all things work together for good to them that love God*…First, the Apostle says *all things*. He excepts nothing. All the events of Providence, whether fortunate or unfortunate, everything that has to do with health or wealth or

---

[96] Juan Lozano, "Saint Teresa Benedicta (Edith) Stein Serves the Church," *Carmel Clarion* Volume XXXVI, No. 4 (Fall 2020): 9.

Epilogue

reputation; every condition of life, all the different interior states through which we may have to pass—desolations, dryness, disgust, weariness, temptations—all this is to be for the advantage of those who love God; and more than this—even our faults, even our sins.

We must be resolved never to offend God willfully; but if unfortunately we do offend Him, our very offenses, our very crimes, may be made use of for our advantage, if we really love God. We have only to remember [King] David, we have only to remember Saint Peter, whose sins served only to make them holier afterward—that is to say, more humble, more grateful to God, more full of love.

All things work together for good. It is not a temporal good, not an earthly good....We must therefore believe...that our true good and our true advantage is found in the events of Divine Providence...although often we cannot understand what God means to do with us....But all these divine arrangements are a good only for those who love God—those who are ready to sacrifice to Him everything without exception.[97]

---

[97] Father Jean-Nicolas Grou, S. J., as found in *Magnificat* magazine, Vol. 22, No. 11, 402-403.

Epilogue

This is how I try to view my illness, and I have seen the truth of it throughout these trials. He has brought about personal spiritual growth, closeness to family and friends, and great gratitude for His blessings. An adaptation of 2 Corinthians 4:6-18 could read: "Therefore, I am not discouraged; rather, although my outer self is wasting away, my inner self is being renewed day by day. For this momentary light affliction is producing for me an eternal weight of glory beyond all comparison, as I look not to what is seen but to what is unseen; for what is seen is transitory, but what is unseen is eternal."

Since my diagnosis, God has brought some healing to my family—though we still have a ways to go and I pray for this every day. The effects of Tim's harshness years ago still linger, but hope for reconciliation remains. The sorrow and regret in my heart for the wounds my children carry is deep.

One day I hope there will be a broader understanding of those years following Ed's death, understanding not only of what difficulties the children were enduring and the emotional burdens I carried, but also what a challenging undertaking it was for Tim to step into our tight-knit family, what courage it required. Yet he never showed the least hesitation nor uncertainty and was eager to try to be a good stepfather. In numerous ways, he was. He spent time with the children and taught them many things. He was an example of generosity,

Epilogue

of prayerfulness, of hard work and responsibility—all manly qualities worth emulating. Sadly, his temper and harshness tarnished these lessons and I was not the strong helpmate that he needed to realize this. Because of my feelings of low self-worth, I did not have the fortitude to stand against his failings. Throughout my life, I have struggled to assert myself in healthy ways. But with God's grace, even our weaknesses and sins can serve to make us, as Fr. Grou's earlier meditation stated, more holier, "more humble, more grateful to God, more full of love."

My illness has given Tim the opportunity to become the hero that he is. He demonstrates Jesus' words: "If then, your Lord and Teacher, have washed your feet, you also ought to wash one another's feet. For I have given you an example, that you also should do as I have done to you" (John 13:14-15). "Whoever would be great among you must be your servant, and whoever would be first among you must be slave of all. For the Son of man also came not to be served but to serve..." (Mark 10:43-45). Tim has cared for me with tenderness and strength, showering me with compassion and love. Is this not one of the purposes of marriage? "Man and woman were made for each other…[God] created them to be a communion of persons, in which each can be a 'helpmate' to the other, for they are equal as persons...and complementary as masculine and feminine."[98] The sacrament of Matrimony is "directed towards the salvation of others; if [it] contributes as well to personal salvation, it is through *service to others* that [it] does so."[99] The "grace proper to the sacrament of Matrimony is intended to perfect the couple's love and to strengthen their indissoluble unity. By this grace they 'help one another to attain holiness in their married life....' "[100] Tim is helping me to attain holiness by his example of love and service; I pray that I am in some way helping him as well.

When I think about dying and going to meet our Lord, I hope also to be reunited with my dear Ed, and to one day welcome Tim and my family into eternity as well. I hope Tim and I will continue our singing together—we sang at his brother's funeral and at our bishop's consecration, and every day he harmonizes with me when we pray Morning and Evening Prayer—and maybe Ed and the children will sing with us in heaven!

A powerful definition of love is to want the ultimate good for another person. And the ultimate good is to be together with the Holy Trinity for eternity. This is what it means to die a happy death: to die in God's grace so as to be with Him for

---

[98] *Catechism of the Catholic Church*, 372.

[99] Ibid, 1534.

[100] Ibid, 1641.

Epilogue

all eternity. How does one die in God's grace? By living a life of faith and prayer, receiving the Anointing of the Sick and the Eucharist, and seeking forgiveness from God (through Confession) and forgiving one another. Family and loved ones can assist a dying person to overcome temptations against faith, despair, impatience, vainglory, and avarice...tactics Satan uses to battle for his possession of the soul. Prayers and proclamations of faith, hope, and love assist the person to experience a holy and happy death.[101]

St. Junipero Serra, the "Apostle of California," said, "Life is uncertain and, in fact, may be very brief. If we compare it with eternity, we will clearly realize that it cannot be but more than an instant. A happy death of all the things of life is our principal concern. For if we attain that, it matters little if we lose all the rest. But if we do not attain that, nothing else will be of any value."[102]

"For me to live is Christ, and to die is gain."
~ Philippians 1:21

Our Lady of Mt. Carmel, pray for us.

---

[101] Brother Columba Thomas, OP, MD, *The Art of Dying—A New Annotated Translation* (Philadelphia, PA: The National Catholic Bioethics Center, 2021).

[102] Ronda DeSola Chervin, *Quotable Saints* (Oak Lawn, IL: CMJ Marian Publishers, 1992), 49.

Appendix One

Ed Stuart's Family Tree

This is based solely on my memory, thus quite incomplete and/or inaccurate.

EDWARD RAYMOND STUART, JR. 1948-2003
Husband of Fae Denise Hampshire Stuart Presley 1978-2003
Children: Joseph Todd (2/26/1980), Heidi Fae (10/7/1982), Rachel Claire (7/23/1984), Lincoln Charles (3/29/1988), Ian Edward Campion (12/2/1995)

Edward's parents:
EDWARD RAYMOND STUART, SR. and MARY GERALDINE HOLCOMB
Children: Susan Marie, Edward Raymond, Jr.

Edward's sister:
SUSAN STUART BRITTEN, Husband Jack
Children: Dennis, Kevin, David

Edward Raymond Stuart, Sr.'s parents:
EDWARD STUART and LEAH BOUTHELIERRE
from Fall River, MA to Detroit MI to Grand Rapids, MI
Children: Pat, "Pep," Edward

Appendix One

PAT STUART McDIARMOD, Husband Rod
Children: Melissa, an M.D.

"PEP" STUART, a nurse

Mary Holcomb's parents:
FLOYD HOLCOMB and MAMIE ANDERSON from Tustin, MI
Children: Fales (died in WWII), Mary, Ardyth
ARDYTH ANDERSON, husband Karl
Children: John, Terry, Randy

Appendix Two

Bible Quiz for Bible Christians

Dear Brother or Sister in Christ,

The Word is full of beautiful and powerful verses. And, of course, each of us is convinced that our interpretation of those verses is the correct one. But because our minds are frail and fallible, or because of the hardness of our hearts, we often see only what we want to see, and remember only what strikes us as important at the moment. That is why we need to read, reread, and study the Bible continuously with open hearts and minds.

Even if we are assisted by the use of a good commentary, or by the words of skilled teachers, we are seeing the Scripture through someone else's eyes—using their doctrinal "lens." The many and often varying interpretations given by a growing number of self-proclaimed experts who, sometimes, seem to be making it up as they go, should raise a red flag to all Christians. There is but one, objective Truth and one Spirit. The Spirit can not contradict Himself or in any way be divided. Truth does not suddenly change or evolve, though our understanding of it may develop and grow. Logically and spiritually we know that two radically different opinions on

Appendix Two

important issues such as *baptismal regeneration, eternal security, abortion, cloning, contraception, euthanasia, the Trinity, suicide, justification, predestination, the atonement, homosexuality, etc.* can't both be correct. False doctrines can be spiritually dangerous—even fatal (I Timothy 4:16). Such doctrinal differences are rampant in our somewhat dysfunctional Christian family which is made up of over 20,000 known sectarian groups.

Everyone is "convicted" that he or she is doctrinally correct, and claims that the Spirit has led him or her to truth, but some are undoubtedly wrong, though all are using the same Bible. Would God leave us marooned in a sea of doctrinal Babel? Of course not. He gave the Church a teaching authority. Which Church has it? Whose lens is the right one? Ponder those things as you take this quiz, which may bring up some teachings that you may have missed in your Bible reading, or that some of your preachers may have neglected—or ignored.

QUIZ

1. In the New Testament, Paul states that _____ is the "pillar and foundation of truth."
a) faith
b) the Lord
c) Scripture

d) the Church

e) grace

2. From Acts through Revelation, there is only *one* direct extended quote taken from the four gospels (Matthew, Mark, Luke, John). Where is the quote and what church practice or issue does it refer to?

3. Name a verse of the Bible in which the words "faith" and "alone" both appear.

4. According to Peter, what must we add to our faith to make our election sure?

a) Nothing

b) Grace

c) Prophecy

d) Self-control, perseverance, godliness

5. True or False: Christ's imputed righteousness "cloaks" us from God's wrath such that we do not actually have to become transformed in holiness to be saved.

6. If we escape damnation by knowing our Lord and Savior Jesus Christ, what happens if we leave the path of righteousness?

a) Nothing (we have eternal security).

b) We are even worse off unless we repent.

7. True or False: Christ sits in triumph at His Father's right hand and has no further priestly sacrificial role to play

because what He has done on Calvary is finished and all sins are forgiven.

8. What action, according to Scripture, causes us to eat and drink judgment on ourselves by sinning against the Body and Blood of Jesus, and could even cause us to suffer bodily harm?

9. True or False: Those who know the Lord but have sinned may lose some reward but will not in any way suffer God's justice when they die.

10. What person, place, or thing in Scripture is described here?
- A holy vessel that held the bread of life
- Contained the word of God
- Before which someone leapt
- Was greeted with, "How can the _____ come to me?"
- Was a blessing to a household in the hills of Judea for three months.

11. Where in the Bible are we warned about the difficulty of understanding certain Scriptures that some people distort to their destruction?

12. Name five objects used as channels of God's healing grace in the New Testament.

Appendix Two

13. True or False: Requesting intercessory prayer from another violates the principal of Christ being the sole mediator. (I Timothy 2:5)

14. "Therefore, brethren, stand fast, and hold the _____ which ye have been taught, whether by word, or our epistle." (King James Version)

15. What person has a name that means "rock" in Aramaic (*kepha*) and Greek (*petra*), and was given the "keys" to a kingdom, as was Eliakim the prime minister of the house of David? (Isaiah 22:20-22)

16. Where in Scripture does it say that Scripture is the *only* source of Truth for Christians?

ANSWERS:

1. d) the Church (**I Timothy 3:15**)
2. See **I Corinthians 11:24-25** concerning the Lord's Supper, the Eucharist
3. Only one verse: **James 2:24:** "You see that a person is justified by what he does and not by faith alone." Luther added the word "alone" to **Romans 3:28**. It is not in the original manuscripts.
4. d) **2 Peter 1:5-10**
5. False. **Ephesians 4:22-32**

Appendix Two

6. b) **2 Peter 2:20-22** and **1 John 1:9**
7. False. The blood of Christ has redeemed us from the curse of Adam's sin by Grace, but we must work out our salvation in fear and trembling **(Philippians 2:12)**. After we are baptized in faith, sins committed must be repented of, for we must be holy as God is holy **(Hebrews 12:14)**. The power and eternal efficacy of Calvary in forgiveness of those sins derives from Jesus' eternal priesthood and ongoing intercession on our behalf, offering continuously the death he suffered once. **1 John 2:2:** "But if anybody does sin, we have one who speaks to the Father in our defense—Jesus Christ, the Righteous One. He is the atoning sacrifice for our sins." The Catholic Mass is an earthly reflection of and an awesome participation in this re-presentation of Christ's sacrifice to the Father in heaven by His Church, His beloved! **(Hebrews 7:25; Hebrews 8: 1-3; Hebrews 13:10)**
8. **1 Corinthians 11:26-30.** Eating and drinking of the Lord's Supper in an unworthy manner.
9. False. **Mathew 12:36:** "But I tell you that men will have to give account on the day of judgment for every careless word they have spoken." Also **Luke 12:47-48**: "That servant will be beaten with many blows." **Matthew 18:34:** "In anger his master turned him over to the jailers to be tortured, until he should pay back all he owed." **Colossians 3:25**: "Anyone who

does wrong will be repaid for his wrong, and there is no favoritism." See also **1 Thessalonians 4:6.**

10. Both Mary and the Ark of the Covenant (see especially **2 Samuel 6:9-16** and **Luke 1:43-56**). The Church's high esteem for Mary parallels the Jews' reverence for the Ark—a type of Mary. As the *Ark of the New Covenant,* she was created and crafted by God using spiritual gold to be a holy and fitting vessel to nurture, cherish, and serve His (and her) divine Son, Jesus Christ.

11. **2 Peter 3:16** concerning Paul's writings.

12. Handkerchiefs, aprons, shadows, oil, mud (**Mark 6:13; John 9:6; Acts 5:15; Acts 19:12**). C.

13. False. **1 Timothy 2:1; Revelation 5:8**

14. Tradition: **2 Thessalonians 2:15**

15. Peter. **Matthew 16:19** shows Peter as a visible rock on the foundation of Christ, who becomes the "prime minister" for the Kingdom of the Son of David with authority to decide doctrinal issues for the whole Church. (e.g. **Acts 15:7 ff**).

16. Nowhere. Neither Scripture nor the early Church ever taught this doctrine. This in no way implies that Scripture is not profitable, useful, and inerrant as in **2 Timothy 3:16**.

Appendix Two

Do some of these verses have a Catholic "ring" to them? Yes, they do, and so do many others. The Christian Church is 2000 years old. Most of the 20,000 Protestant sectarian groups are less than 100. Only the Catholic Church has been there the whole time. Yes, many Church leaders have sinned and betrayed the Lord. That started in apostolic times and continues to this day. But do you really think the Holy Spirit abandoned the Church for 1500 years awaiting the Reformation? The Lord did not throw us an instruction manual without giving us a Church, guided by the Spirit, as a guarantor of correct interpretation. Who could be better at interpreting the love letters of the Groom than the Bride? You know what many Protestants say about the Catholic Church; find out what the Catholic Church says.

—Ed Stuart

Appendix Three

My Father's Briefcase

Joseph T. Stuart

The month of April always brings to mind my father, Edward Stuart. It was the month when he entered the world in 1948 and the month when he left it in 2003. My father was respected by all who knew him for his unusually curious and open mind and his robust intellectual charity. He was one of the most respected professors at Ferris State University, where he taught for fourteen years. His students came to his wake. His colleagues in electrical engineering donated their sick leave and volunteered regular deductions from their paychecks to help our family. Dad finished the school year and then took ill and never returned, so his office had to be cleaned out. I ended up with his briefcase. I have kept it these several years and recently opened it to sort carefully through its contents.

One of the clasps of this black, hard-shell briefcase no longer functions. But its contents reveal much about the man who carried it to work. As an historian, I am constantly fascinated by what primary sources reveal about human life in the past. Letters, manuscripts, journals, memoirs, reports, and published books are ways of seeing the feats and failures of those who lived before us. This briefcase opens up the world of my father during his last months of health in a way that little else can.

He did not always carry a briefcase. Dad was known early in his employment at Ferris as the professor who carried a five-gallon bucket. Our family had a lot of buckets lying around because they served to transport kindling into the house for the woodstove. Since Dad was thoroughly non-conventional and cared little how others saw him, he thought that a large pail would serve just fine to transport his calculator, pens, graph paper, and engineering textbooks.

Eventually, he acquired the old, black briefcase and would carry it to work every day. That was literally true, for with a half-mile long driveway that often drifted full of snow during long Michigan winters, our family was often snowbound. Dad would walk out to the car parked on the road and then trudge home at the end of the day with his briefcase in one hand and a gallon of milk in the other.

The contents of the briefcase reveal Dad's wide interests. Only a portion of the contents has anything to do directly with his work at the university. He thought of many things on a typical day. There is Dad's witty and provocative sense of humor. I found a droll Dave Barry column on the SAT exam and also a calendar with a random scribble on it that says: "Lawyer = larval form of politician." Then there are several

Appendix Three

copies of a cartoon poking fun at postmodernism: "Breakfast Theory: A Morning Methodology." A cereal box reads, "Post Modern Toasties...Like everything you've had before, all mixed up." Dad wrote a joke that I once told him at the bottom of the cartoon: "As the French say: 'Yes it works in practice, but does it work in theory?'"

Dad seemed to sense that his time was short even before the symptoms of brain cancer suddenly hit him in July 2002. He grew nostalgic. He spent time at the end of his final semester that spring going through old photographs and looking up old friends to try to contact them. In his briefcase I found a handwritten note with the address of one of his old medical school buddies (Dad spent two-and-a-half years in medical school). Then there is the obituary of the Jesuit priest Anderson Bakewell who held advanced degrees in astronomy, mathematics, and philosophy and who was also a member of the Explorer's Club. Dad knew him in Alaska and wrote on the obituary, "Worked for him 1975/1976 in Delta Junction, Alaska." Why did he scribble that note on the obituary? For whose sake did he write it? Who could he have thought would read it? Dad frequently wrote little notes like that, even as a kid, such as, "Ed was here" on the underside of a table. They were little reminders of his life, as if he wanted others to know that he had passed that way and that his life held a purpose. I once found a note that Dad wrote out in the forest near our

Appendix Three

home. In September 2003, five months after he was gone, I rambled across a birch tree upon which Dad had drawn a heart and the message, "September 2001, Ed loves Fae." I ran home to lead my mother to see it. She wept. He couldn't have expected anyone to ever read it. He just wrote it because...he wanted to. That was the kind of man he was.

Dad admired Fr. Bakewell as a man of God and a man of learning. These two characteristics defined Dad himself, and are seen in his briefcase. There is his New Testament, which Dad frequently read. There is a list of verses for memorization, the "Hail Mary" in Spanish, and several pages of research on the alleged Marian apparitions at Medjugorje, where Dad visited during the early 1990s. This love of God accompanied a lifelong passion for learning. His friend Jim Loftis remembered that, "Ed had the only set of 'Encyclopedia Britannica' in the neighborhood. He would read them voraciously and pass along information he learned from these books." The "A" encyclopedia rested near him during his final sickness—next to a book on purgatory and a set of German tapes. I found in the briefcase a magazine article on DNA (Dad was fascinated by genetics during his last two years of life). Dad would often work on problems in astronomy as we children were growing up. In his briefcase I found a piece of graph paper on which Dad was trying to work out the most likely date for the birth of Christ using

Appendix Three

historical and astronomical evidence. He would have appreciated what Galileo wrote in his 1613 letter to Castelli: "Sacred Scripture and nature proceed equally from the Divine Word."

Dad kept up on news and contemporary concerns. I found critical responses to the outbreak of news reports on the priest scandals in the spring of 2002. Dad had studied Russian in college and in his briefcase I found an appeal letter for Aid to the Church in Russia. There were two other charities that he was evidently interested in: one for the restoration of a church structure in Stuart, Iowa, where he had once visited, and the other for aid to the people of Afghanistan.

I found personal and poignant evidences of my father's last concerns as a working man. There are three copies of a photograph of our family. There is a printout of the lyrics to "Don Quixote," a song by Gordon Lightfoot, one of his favorite musicians. Dad sometimes saw himself as Lightfoot's Don Quixote, a lone wanderer through life. There is a copy of his resume, which I am glad of because I would not have had a copy otherwise. I was moved when I came across a handout from a lecture I gave at the Russell Kirk Center in February 2002 on "Progress and Religion," a book by the English historian of culture Christopher Dawson (1889-1970). Dad must have been interested in the topic for there is in his briefcase the first page (where is the rest?) of Joseph

Koterski's article on Dawson called "Religion as the Root of Culture." He underlined Dawson's phrase "religion is the key of history." My father did not live to see me mature into the historian and scholar of Dawson and early twentieth-century Britain that I have become. However, he was there at the beginning and was fascinated by the history of Christianity, as his briefcase testifies.

An historian reconstructs the past out of the debris that is "cast up by the sea from the wrecks of countless ages" (Herbert Butterfield). All of these papers and articles in the small confines of a briefcase reveal the essence of my father. His quiet example of a life of prayer and intelligence has inspired my life.

Appendix Four

A Tribute to Edward Stuart from his family, Christmas 2003.

Ian Stuart, age 8

Dad was very good to me! I miss him very much! I always ask him to pray for me. Sometimes I cry because I miss him. But I am always happy because I think Dad is in heaven! I loved Dad so much! Good bye Dad. He is always in my heart. I always think about Dad. I will offer it up to God that my dad is gone. Dad, please pray for me.

Lincoln Stuart, age 15

I was taught many things by my dad. These things range from earthy things, trivial things and not so trivial things. Humor was one of Dad's strong points. He always enjoyed a good laugh and witty jokes. Consequently, some of the lessons he taught me are quite humorous. However, he was not solely comprised of humor as to make him a "push-over" and hollow inside. His character was well-balanced in the traits of humor and dead-seriousness. Thus, lessons he taught me range from humorous ones to the utmost of seriousness.

One lesson I was taught at a young and innocent age. I couldn't have been more than four years old when my family had decided to take a vacation to Montana. This vacation found us trudging up mountains, looking for plausible real-estate to buy and, of course, sleeping in tents. One night in the crammed dome tent, I decided I needed to visit the outhouse. So, it being dark, I appealed to Dad to take me and protect me from the "potty-monsters." He, not wanting to get out of his sleeping bag, groggily told me to "just go." Dad meant for me to step outside the tent and go behind a nearby bush or tree. However, I (being very young as I said above) interpreted "just go" to mean just that! So, relieved that I wouldn't have to walk all the way to the frightening and dark outhouse, I proceeded to do my business right there and right then...inside the tent!!! As you can imagine, I will never forget the lesson Dad taught me that night: NEVER URINATE INSIDE A TENT!

One goal that Dad has unknowingly set for me is my striving to become a safe driver. Just recently I was involved in my first (and hopefully last) "fender-bender" with another vehicle. This incident reminded me of how safe a driver Dad really was. Never was Dad careless or reckless when it came to driving. In fact, I never remember even being pulled over by a policeman when Dad was driving. My sister Heidi and I both agree that since Dad has passed away, we haven't felt *really* safe and confident when riding in a car (don't tell my Mom and brother who do most of the driving these days!)

Appendix Four

Dad has also taught me that I should never lose hope...especially when it came to schoolwork. Dad (in my mind) was as close as a human could become to "all-knowing." There was almost no subject that he didn't at least know a minimal amount about (okay so maybe he didn't know too much about baking pastries or French manicures). As I look at his book shelf at this moment, I see such titles as *Fundamentals of Genetics, Electromechanics, Basic Radio, How Windows Works, Calculus, The Astronomer's Manual, Carpentry, Small Business Management, Handbook for Boy Scouts, The Outline of History*, and many more wide ranges of titles. His knowledge ran from photography to astronomy, from human anatomy to calculus, from building log cabins to repairing small engines, from raising a family to electronics, and, of course, he knew way *too much* about snow blowing a ½ mile driveway! Whenever I was mystified by some aspect of elementary algebra, I ran to Dad for a complete lesson. The lesson began with some good-natured raillery consisting of something like, *"You can't do that??? Ha ha ha!"* All in good fun, of course. Then he would begin the long and laborious process of drilling into my ungrasping mind simple aspects of elementary algebra, such things like x is, in fact, not a letter but an unknown number (as you can see, I amazingly enough somehow managed to retain these simple aspects in my memory, much to the credit of Dad)! Always at the end of the lesson I would be able to walk away with the aspect firmly concreted in my mind, and a pile of papers with detailed schematics (depending on the lesson) filled with x's and y's, plenty of equal signs, and/or perfectly drawn triangles and 3D cylinders with area, circumference etc. penned in the proper places. Yes, Dad was an excellent teacher, something his students at Ferris State University assert, and, his own troop of students at home also testify to.

Dad always encouraged me too (and indeed still does to this day). Not one for inaction, Dad was always in the front lines of battle. You probably never knew that Dad was a high-ranking officer in the military, did you? Okay, so maybe not in the U.S. military, or any other temporal military, but spiritually speaking he must have ranked at least Rear Admiral (Upper Half). When faced with a situation where he could either combat the wrong thinking of an individual or remain silent...the choice for him was obvious; actually, there really wasn't a choice. He would be up in arms in a moment's notice, and always he knew of the biggest guns he could bring to bear upon his enemy. Such big bore guns as C. S. Lewis, Pat Madrid and *Gray's Anatomy*. Yes, Dad loved to give agnostics and atheists the ol' one two punch of the complexity of the mechanics of a cell and its incorporation into the human body as counter arguments. As you can imagine, nobody long withstood the withering salvos Dad fired!

Appendix Four

Dad was an incredible individual whom I shall never, ever forget. I feel so blessed to have had him in my life for fifteen whole years. If I can remember and follow Dad's legacy in my future life, it will be a sole "life-line" leading to salvation. Thank you, Dad, for your unselfishness in leaving me, and us, such a life-line.

Rachel Stuart, age 19

My daddy will always live on in my memory as my friend, protector, and teacher. He taught me to be humble by his example. He was quiet at times and didn't make an exhibit of himself, which would have been so easy to do, given that he knew so much and had done so much. He and I were very alike in many ways. We both loved the wilderness and wild places, we both loved to wander off alone and think, talking to ourselves. Daddy truly loved all people, but especially those less fortunate than himself, or looked down on by others. One time Dad was walking down the street in the winter, and seeing a man walking past, cold and with no coat on, gave him his vest. So he himself finished his walk in the cold.

It is the little things that I think of the most and make me miss him. I went to school at Ferris State University for a couple of years while my dad taught there. I got to spend so much time with him. I wish I had appreciated it more then. He and I would walk around campus, and sometimes, when we came to a street, he would take my hand and grin at me, challenging me to see if I was embarrassed! I didn't care that a bunch of college students saw me holding my dad's hand crossing the street, I was so proud to be with him. I was always his little girl, and I liked it that way. I told the story at his funeral of the time when we had driven to church in the winter, and by the time we got back home, our driveway was filled in by five foot snowdrifts. So we parked at the end of the driveway, and started walking. I, being a little lass, had on a skirt and had bare legs and not very good shoes. So I floundered in the snowdrifts, crying and freezing. But I had nothing to fear, my big, heroic daddy scooped me up in his arms, and, though tired himself, carried me the long half mile through the drifts back to our house.

The last real walk I took with Dad was in September of last year [2002]. He had had his surgery, and was not yet on his treatment, so he was thinking very clearly still. He took me on a walk down the driveway with him (so many problems have been faced on that half mile stretch of two-track.) He tried to tell me that he probably wasn't going to make it through this. I didn't listen to him; I shoved it back in his face. I didn't want to believe that he would die, and I wanted him to keep trying. He ended by telling me how much he loved me, was proud of me, and, even if he wasn't always there, he'd always look after his little girl. He's kept his promise. He isn't

Appendix Four

here, but I know that he's taking care of me, he's proud of me. At school sometimes, I get so frustrated because I want to ask him a question about philosophy, or logic, but I can't because he's not just a phone call away anymore.

This is going to be a hard Christmas without him. Just two years ago, what an eternity, he bought me something that I still have. I'm kind of silly and old-fashioned, but I love anything old or antique. Daddy knew this, so he got me an antique iron that you heat up on the stove. Most daughters would have been extremely disappointed by such a silly gift, but it was a treasure to me, because I know how much thought and love went into it. Only he really understood that about me, and that little gift was an acknowledgment of that bond between us. So, Christmas will not be the same. Daddy won't be sitting in the rocking chair, with his leg up on the arm of it, watching his little brood gleefully opening their gifts. Once in a while receiving one himself, usually something kind of strange from one of us kids, or sometimes a new tool that he bought for himself because that's the only way he could get it! He won't be there to kiss goodnight, say, "Merry Christmas" to, and, "Thanks for all the presents today!" Yet, I suppose he can still hear me, and that he'd want me to say, "Goodnight Daddy, I love you, and thank you for all of your gifts!"

Appendix Four

Heidi was already married and had left home, so she had not written for this family Christmas letter.

Joseph Stuart, age 23

We Stuarts love so many of the Old Ways, of old fashioned fun, old fashioned food, and the truths of authentic religion, all of which express so well the realities of genuine human living. *Reality*...? The world today is so infatuated with the unreal, the twisting bodies and flashing lights of the dance club, or the hectic rush of cell phones and business suits. But I love the world, that world of nature and of family, hard work, even suffering....I love the world where real fires heat the home and real people inhabit it, people who have something to think about, and who care to learn new knowledge of that world, and of ordering it and redeeming it.

Our parish priest recently challenged the congregation to think about our core values. This is one of mine: a love for the *real*, and a desire to cultivate human life that befriends that reality. My father taught me this. Sure, he was interested in GPS and taught electronics, but his heart was always elsewhere, somewhere deeper and more natural, perhaps on the trap lines of his friends in Alaska or in the forest near our home. His was the heart of a pilgrim, ever restless in this present world; he disbelieved the "dreams of avarice." He appreciated many modern advances and possessions, but was

Appendix Four

not possessed by them. He cared little about clothing, and was generous with money. He was able to get his head above material things and so was free to see reality in a true light.

Dad always loved nature, a good hike, and the independence of a rustic way of life. He cultivated this trait in his many excursions to the Rockies, but especially in his wanderings in Alaska where he built a cabin on a remote island in the Tanana River and helped an old lady cut up a drowned moose with a chain saw. Dad was always a great walker; he frequented our long driveway of the hayfield hill and its marvelous view. He reflected much, and no doubt prayed, while outdoors.

Dad sought learning, often for its own sake. He delighted not just in *experiencing* reality but in *understanding* it, whether that be through astronomy, genetics, microbiology, advanced mathematics, history, or the mysteries of the Faith. Such interests as these meant that Dad enjoyed silence, that best friend of the thinking man. He eschewed the modern rush to be "distracted from distractions" by the noise and the silliness that kills the mind. To seek to understand reality, the mysteries of nature, of man, and of God—this my father taught me. Also, time. Earthly ambition meant little to Dad. He would spend hours with us children, in conversing or explaining or just walking and often reading aloud. He loved us and he loved the world, and it was the setting aside of time for human interaction that passed on Dad's values to us, the next generation.

Dad's was a sacramental life of a mysterious harmony between the man of rustic loves, and the man of the university professorship; the man of faith, and the man of study. His was a quiet but powerful legacy of the love of *life*, the examined life, the life worth living, and supernatural life.

Dad would not like what we are thinking about him here; he would say that we have exaggerated and try to distract our attention by telling us of something interesting he just read; the simple man wastes not time on self-congratulation. But it is true, and I have written it.

Edward Stuart, my father and my friend, I miss you and I salute you.

Fae Stuart

I am so thankful for being Ed's wife for 25 years. I learned so many things from him and was given so much that I cannot mention it all here. It seems every day I remember something that Ed taught me. I learned how to read maps from Ed. He opened my eyes to the wonders of nature and of our country by traveling throughout the USA with me and our family. He taught me about birds and how to enjoy learning about them. He taught me how to spot a false argument, and how to logically think through rebuttals. He kept me from getting too mired down in routine and added interest and excitement to our lives. He had this subtle sense of humor and the kids and I chuckle often now when we think of the funny things he would do or say. (He thought it was a great joke to wear one of my breastfeeding shirts to work in front of all his students!) Ed knew so much about so many subjects that I learned to trust him whenever I had a question about literally anything. It was extremely rare that I would ask him a question and not get at least an educated guess!

Ed lived his faith in unobtrusive, but powerful ways. He balanced my keen sense of justice with a good amount of mercy and showed me how important it is to refrain from judging others' intentions. He showed me generosity every day of our marriage—he continually gave and gave and gave to me and to our children. He respected me and listened to me, enjoying our conversation and valuing my opinions. He supported me and helped me, from the intensity of nursing school in our early days to the awesome responsibilities and decision-making of pregnancy and childbearing, to the later challenges of homeschooling five children and nurturing teenagers and young adults. Ed was secure in his manhood and did not fear the world. He knew what is important in life and had his priorities in the right order. The most amazing thing was that this wonderful man loved me with all of my weaknesses! The fruit of our love, our children, are exquisite gifts from my husband, for which I thank God every day. And the first thing that attracted me to him back in 1976 was his quiet, steady faith in God and His Church—which will remain forever the most important gift he gave to me.

Appendix Five

Favorite Scripture Verses

John 1:1-18 — In the beginning was the Word, and the Word was with God, and the Word was God. He was in the beginning with God. All things came to be through him, and without him nothing came to be. What came to be through him was life, and this life was the light of the human race; the light shines in the darkness, and the darkness has not overcome it.

A man named John was sent from God. He came for testimony, to testify to the light, so that all might believe through him. He was not the light, but came to testify to the light. The true light, which enlightens everyone, was coming into the world.

He was in the world, and the world came to be through him, but the world did not know him. He came to what was his own, but his own people did not accept him.
But to those who did accept him he gave power to become children of God, to those who believe in his name, who were born not by natural generation nor by human choice nor by a man's decision but of God.

And the Word became flesh and made his dwelling among us, and we saw his glory, the glory as of the Father's only Son, full of grace and truth.

John testified to him and cried out, saying, "This was he of whom I said, 'The one who is coming after me ranks ahead of me because he existed before me.'" From his fullness we have all received, grace in place of grace, because while the law was given through Moses, grace and truth came through Jesus Christ. No one has ever seen God. The only Son, God, who is at the Father's side, has revealed him.

Psalm 25:1-21 — To thee, O Lord, I lift up my soul. O my God, in thee I trust, let me not be put to shame; let not my enemies exult over me.

Yea, let none that wait for thee be put to shame; let them be ashamed who are wantonly treacherous.

Appendix Five

Make me to know thy ways, O Lord; teach me thy paths. Lead me in thy truth, and teach me, for thou art the God of my salvation; for thee I wait all the day long.

Be mindful of thy mercy, O Lord, and of thy steadfast love, for they have been from of old. Remember not the sins of my youth, or my transgressions; according to thy steadfast love remember me, for thy goodness' sake, O Lord!

Good and upright is the Lord; therefore he instructs sinners in the way. He leads the humble in what is right, and teaches the humble his way. All the paths of the Lord are steadfast love and faithfulness, for those who keep his covenant and his testimonies.

For thy name's sake, O Lord, pardon my guilt, for it is great. Who is the man that fears the Lord? Him will he instruct in the way that he should choose. He himself shall abide in prosperity, and his children shall possess the land. The friendship of the Lord is for those who fear him, and he makes known to them his covenant. My eyes are ever toward the Lord, for he will pluck my feet out of the net.

Turn thou to me, and be gracious to me; for I am lonely and afflicted. Relieve the troubles of my heart, and bring me out of my distresses. Consider my affliction and my trouble, and forgive all my sins.

Consider how many are my foes, and with what violent hatred they hate me. Oh guard my life, and deliver me; let me not be put to shame, for I take refuge in thee. May integrity and uprightness preserve me, for I wait for thee.

I John 4:10 — In this is love, not that we loved God but that He loved us and sent His Son to be the expiation for our sins.

Matthew 8:27 — And the men marveled, saying, "What sort of man is this, that even winds and sea obey Him?"

Psalm 46:10 — "Be still, and know that I am God."

Philippians 2:3-11 — Do nothing out of selfishness or out of vainglory; rather, humbly regard others as more important than yourselves, each looking out not for his own interests, but [also] everyone for those of others. Have among yourselves the same

Appendix Five

attitude that is also yours in Christ Jesus, Who, though he was in the form of God, did not regard equality with God something to be grasped.

Rather, he emptied himself, taking the form of a slave, coming in human likeness; and found human in appearance, he humbled himself, becoming obedient to death, even death on a cross.

Because of this, God greatly exalted him and bestowed on him the name that is above every name, that at the name of Jesus every knee should bend, of those in heaven and on earth and under the earth, and every tongue confess that Jesus Christ is Lord, to the glory of God the Father.

Philippians 4:6, 7 — Have no anxiety at all, but in everything, by prayer and petition, with thanksgiving, make your requests known to God. Then the peace of God that surpasses all understanding will guard your hearts and minds in Christ Jesus.

Colossians 3:12-17 — Put on then, as God's chosen ones, holy and beloved, heartfelt compassion, kindness, humility, gentleness, and patience, bearing with one another and forgiving one another, if one has a grievance against another; as the Lord has forgiven you, so must you also do. And over all these put on love, that is, the bond of perfection. And let the peace of Christ control your hearts, the peace into which you were also called in one body. And be thankful. Let the word of Christ dwell in you richly, as in all wisdom you teach and admonish one another, singing psalms, hymns, and spiritual songs with gratitude in your hearts to God. And whatever you do, in word or in deed, do everything in the name of the Lord Jesus, giving thanks to God the Father through him.

2 Timothy 4:2-5 — Proclaim the word; be persistent whether it is convenient or inconvenient; convince, reprimand, encourage through all patience and teaching. For the time will come when people will not tolerate sound doctrine but, following their own desires and insatiable curiosity, will accumulate teachers and will stop listening to the truth and will be diverted to myths. But you, be self-possessed in all circumstances; put up with hardship; perform the work of an evangelist; fulfill your ministry.

Hebrews 13:14-16 — For here we have no lasting city, but we seek the one that is to come. Through him [then] let us continually offer God a sacrifice of praise, that is, the fruit of lips that confess his name. Do not neglect to do good and to share what you have; God is pleased by sacrifices of that kind.

I John 1:9 — If we acknowledge our sins, he is faithful and just and will forgive our sins and cleanse us from every wrongdoing.

John 14:1-6 — "Let not your hearts be troubled; believe in God, believe also in me. In my Father's house are many rooms; if it were not so, would I have told you that I go to prepare a place for you? And when I go to prepare a place for you, I will come again and will take you to myself, that where I am you may be also. And you know the way where I am going."

Thomas said to him, "Lord, we do not know where you are going; how can we know the way?" Jesus said to him, "I am the way, and the truth, and the life; no one comes to the Father, but by me."

Psalms 51:1-2 — Have mercy on me, O God, according to thy steadfast love; according to thy abundant mercy blot out my transgressions. Wash me thoroughly from my iniquity, and cleanse me from my sin!

Psalms 51:10-12 — Create in me a clean heart, O God, and put a new and right spirit within me. Cast me not away from thy presence, and take not thy holy Spirit from me. Restore unto me the joy of thy salvation, and uphold me with a willing spirit.

Matthew 28:6 — He is not here; for he has risen, as he said.

Isaiah 26:12 — O Lord, you mete out peace to us, for it is you who have accomplished all we have done.

Ephesians 3:20-21 — Now to him who is able to accomplish far more than all we ask or imagine, by the power at work within us, to him be glory in the church and in Christ Jesus to all generations, forever and ever. Amen.

Acknowledgments

With gratitude to those who read this manuscript and gave constructive criticism: Rose Bingham, Cynthia Bockhold, Kay Dowling, Sheila Gutierrez, Janet McKenzie, Msgr. Michael Steber, and Lydia Tiseo. Their input has been extremely valuable and appreciated!

With deep love and thankfulness to my parents, who enriched my life with gifts I am still discovering.

To my five children: each of you has blessed me and caused my heart to expand in love. I am so proud of all of you, and I love you very much. Please forgive me for the ways I have sinned against you in "what I have done and in what I have failed to do." Thank you for your prayers for me.

Joseph, thank you for upholding me after Dad died, and for always honoring me. Thank you for your bold faithfulness, your steady hand, your love for life. I treasure the ways you share the many gifts in your life with me.

Heidi, thank you for the sunshine you bring to life and for your generosity. Thank you for all you have taught me. You are a lovely battle-maiden in pursuit of the good, the true, and the beautiful.

Rachel, thank you for your tender compassion and self-giving love. With what grace you cared for our family and

Acknowledgments

me in times of need. You are a beautiful woman of strength and understanding, perseverance and patience.

Lincoln, thank you for your courage, your thoughtfulness of others, and your humility. Thank you for honoring our family with your military service. Your life of surprises has brought me wonder and joy.

Ian, thank you for helping me grow in humility and virtue. Your fearlessness and conscientious commitment to duty remind me very much of your father. May his intercession bring us healing and peace.

I am indebted to all those who have prayed and sacrificed for me throughout my life. May God reward their generous love and concern.

And thanks be to God for two remarkable husbands, who have loved me "for better for worse, for richer for poorer, in sickness and in health, until death do us part."

Praise God from whom all blessings flow. Let us praise His name together!